'Et lorsqu'on parlera de la résurrection de Saint-Lô l'Irlande sera toujours à l'honneur'

'And whenever people talk of the resurrection of Saint-Lô Ireland will always deserve special mention'

M. Quévy, *Président du Comité de Défense des Sinistrés de Saint-Lô*

Christmas 1999.

To dear Evelyn,
Thank you for caring so much about the "family" through the years. I hope this book will bring back happy memories of Paddy McW. to you.
Love & best wishes always.
Isabelle.

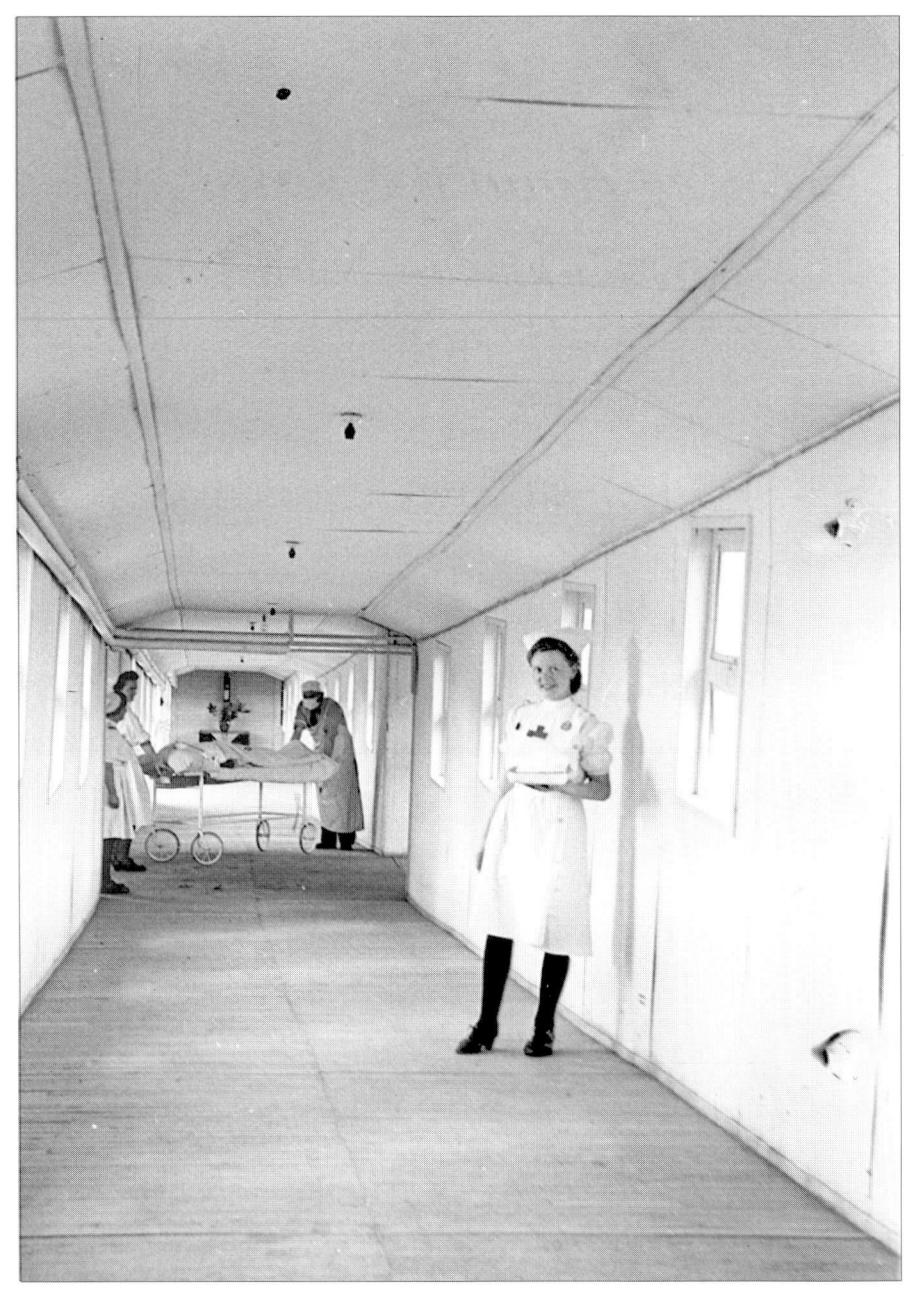

'this domain of white huts with its bright rooms full of flowers'
'cette cité blanche, aux salles claires et fleuries' (Desmond Leahy)

Healing Amid the Ruins
The *hôpital irlandais*, Saint-Lô
(1945–46)

Phyllis Gaffney

A. & A. Farmar

Copyright © Phyllis Gaffney 1999

All rights reserved. No part of this publication may be reproduced in any form or by any means without the prior permission of the publisher.

British Library cataloguing in Publication Data
A CIP catalogue record for this book is available from the British Library

Cover design by Liam Furlong
Designed and set by A. & A. Farmar
Index by Kathy Farmar
Printed and bound by βetaprint

ISBN (PB) 1-899047-33-6

Published by
A. & A. Farmar
Beech House
78 Ranelagh Village
Dublin 6
Ireland
Tel: +353 1 496 3625
Fax: + 353 1 497 0107
Email: afarmar@iol.ie
Web: farmarbooks.com

Contents

Preface	vii
1: Saint-Lô 1944, *capitale des ruines*	1
2: The Irish Red Cross hospital unit	15
3: A hospital of wooden huts	28
4: No ramshackle affair	43
5: The *affaire de l'hôpital irlandais*	57
6: As good as they gave	71
A photographic record The *hôpital irlandais*, Saint-Lô 1945–46: *témoignage photographique*	81
L'hôpital des ruines: les Irlandais à Saint-Lô 1945–46	114
Irish Red Cross staff at the *hôpital irlandais*	145
Notes to the English text	148
Sources and bibliography	166
Index	172

For my parents—Jim,
whom I never knew as a father,
but whose letters from Saint-Lô
started me on the story,
and Ethna, who has played
the role of two parents.

Preface

One cold winter's night in Normandy in 1945, between midnight and dawn, an American military jeep, on its way to Le Havre, was waiting for a ferry to cross the Seine. A line of vehicles was queuing in front of it—British, American, French. The officer in the American jeep noticed that the vehicle just in front of his had a strange registration number, of a kind he had never seen before: neither American, nor British, nor French. Where could it be from?

Curious to investigate, he got out and walked over to the vehicle and, peering more closely in the dark, he realised that it was an Irish ambulance. 'Wonder what the devil the Irish are doing in this thing. I thought they were neutral!' he mused aloud to his driver.

Some days later, a courier turned up at the US base, bearing a written invitation to come and dine with the Irish at their hospital in Saint-Lô, so that the American could see precisely 'just what the devil the Irish were doing' in Normandy. The invitation was signed 'Jim Gaffney'.

That US soldier, Captain Coite Somers, is one of the mythical figures of my childhood. The Irishman driving the ambulance was my father, Dr Jim Gaffney, who worked as pathologist at the Irish Red Cross Hospital in Saint-Lô from August 1945 to August 1946. The two men became close friends. Less than five and a half years later, my father lost his life in the first Aer Lingus air crash in North Wales, on 10 January 1952. I am his posthumous daughter.

Captain Somers continued to correspond for a number of years with my mother, my two brothers and myself. Every Christmas, we looked forward to the arrival of an enormous package from Georgia, full of extraordinary presents, bought for Jim's children by his friend from Normandy.

Healing Amid the Ruins

In a sense, this book represents a repetition of my father's invitation to the Americans. It asks a wider audience to become acquainted with a group of Irish people involved in the reconstruction of a small town in Normandy after the Allied bombings and havoc of the summer of 1944. The story of Saint-Lô's Irish Hospital, which was the first overseas mission of the Irish Red Cross, is not very well known and yet it is of considerable interest from several points of view—medical, social, historical, diplomatic and literary.

To tell the story I have drawn on oral and visual sources, archival material and published and unpublished writings. The research could not have been carried out without the support of a very wide number of people and organisations, in France and in Ireland. My thanks are due, firstly, to Bruno Robin, whose presence in the University College Dublin French Department in 1995–6, was the first link in a chain of contacts. It was he who put me in touch with two women without whose energy and enthusiasm the project to commemorate the Irish Hospital would never have got under way: Madame Jacqueline Fontanel and Madame Marie-Anne Théot, founding members of the Shanaghy Association of Saint-Lô, which is dedicated to fostering links with Ireland.

Many other people in or near Saint-Lô have been kind enough to answer questions, in interviews and by letter, or volunteered information and reminiscences of their own accord: Madame Andrée Blouet, Madame Bernadette Camon, Monsieur Marcel Daguts, Mademoiselle Isabelle de Bonnières, Madame Cécile Delannoë (who died in January 1998), Monsieur Denis de Kergorlay and his aunt, Madame Brigitte de Kergorlay, Madame Rosalie Lecluse, Monsieur Maurice Lerebourg, Madame Lemeray, Monsieur Jean-Jaques Leroy, Monsieur Marcel Menant (who died in December 1998), Madame Simone McKee and Madame Paulette Villechalane. Thanks, too, are due to the committee members of the Shanaghy Association, who made contacts with these people possible.

Preface

Archival assistance was readily provided by the staff of a number of Saint-Lô institutions, including Monsieur Jeanne of the town's Mémorial hospital, Monsieur Jacques Joubin at the Hôtel de Ville, Monsieur Alain Talon of the *Archives Départementales de la Manche* and Monsieur Hubert Godefroy of the *Musée du Bocage Normand* at the Ferme du Bois-Jugan. Elsewhere in France, my thanks are due to Madame Garay of the *Service de Documentation* at the headquarters of the *Croix-Rouge Française*, and to the archival staff at the Quai d'Orsay, in Paris; to Monsieur l'Abbé Couppey of the Diocesan Archives in Coutances; and to Annie Bancroft and Julia McLaren of the *Centre Parisien d'Études et de Documentation pour l'Enseignement et le Rayonnement du Français* in Paris. Catriona Bernard's hospitality in Paris was also much appreciated.

Nearer to home, I wish to express my deepest gratitude to my aunt, Miss Josie Gaffney, who, in keeping her late brother's letters from Saint-Lô, preserved an invaluable written record of daily life at the Irish Hospital. For sundry memories and genealogical assistance, I am also indebted to my mother, Ethna Gaffney.

Inevitably, Samuel Beckett's sojourn in Saint-Lô has attracted others before me, and in this connection I am very grateful to two eminent scholars for their kind encouragement and help: Professor James Knowlson and Professor Eoin O'Brien. For permission to quote from the letters of Beckett, I am grateful to Mr Edward Beckett and the Board of Trinity College, Dublin and for permission to quote from the author's published writings I am grateful to the Samuel Beckett Estate and the Calder Educational Trust.

Many individuals in Ireland and abroad have answered questions, provided information, shared memories and lent photographic and other materials. Amongst these, I am particularly indebted to Nurse Angela Buckley (who died in March 1998) and Dr Desmond Leahy, former director of the hospital. To others who shared first-hand reminiscences I am very grateful, and hope that the following list is comprehensive: Mrs Máire Cruise O'Brien, Mrs Meave Fitzgerald, Mrs Jacqueline MacMahon, Dr Sheila Mulloy, Mrs Margaret O'Loughlin, Mrs Mary Pat O'Malley and Mrs Blánaid O'Rahilly. For more indirect assistance, I wish to thank Mr Aidan Arnold; Mr Tom Arnold; Dr Roger Blaney; Dr Nessa Carroll; Mrs Freddie Corcoran; Dr Eoin Gaffney; Mr Maurice Gaffney; Dr Michael Gaffney; Mrs Maureen Gorman; Dr Tom Gumbrielle; Mrs Simone Hale; Fr Frank Kelly; Mrs Kay Kirwan; Mr Dermot MacDermott; Mrs Treasa McLoughlin; Mrs Isabelle McNicholas; Judge Conor Maguire; Mr Peter Maguire; Mrs Maeve O'Donnell; Mrs Margaret Ó hUadhaigh; Dr Seán Ó Riain; Mr Brian Scott; Mr Cornelius Smith; Professor Louis Smith; Dr Jack Sullivan; Mr Marcus Thompson; Mr Piers Thompson; Ms Rosemary Toner and Miss Bridie Walsh.

For help in attempting to trace—however unsuccessfully—some of the former German prisoners of war who worked at the hospital, I am grateful to Dr Dermot Bradley and Professor John FitzGerald; to Drs Máire Mulloy and Reiner Nolden; and to Hans Christian Oeser. For seeking an American reference, my thanks are due to Dr Bill Williams in Cinncinnati, Ohio. Eithne Fitzgerald and Patrick Honohan have willingly supplied answers to queries on economic history.

I would like to record my gratitude to others deployed in various institutions, from whom I have sought archival, bibliographical and other guidance: Ms Beatrice Doran and Ms Mary O'Doherty, Mercer Library and Ms Kay Kinirons, Faculty of Nursing, Royal College of Surgeons in Ireland; Professor Albert Lovett, History Department, University College Dublin; Ms Rita Collins, Department of Nursing Studies, University College Dublin; Dr Helen O'Neill, Development Studies Centre, University College Dublin; Ms Eiléan Ní Chuilleanáin and Mr David Wheatley, Trinity College Dublin; Ms Catherine Harrison, Mr Pat Hogan and Mr Richie

Preface

Ryan, Irish Red Cross Society; Ms Colette O'Daly, National Library of Ireland; Commandant Peter Young, Irish Military Archives, Cathal Brugha Barracks; Mr Brian Lynch, Archivist, Radio Telefís Éireann; Mr Stephen Connelly and Mr Jeremy Duncan of the A. K. Bell Library, Perth, Scotland; and the staff of the Audio-Visual Centre, University College Dublin; the Central Catholic Library, Dublin; the Irish Architectural Archive; the Manuscripts Room, Trinity College Dublin; and the National Archives of Ireland.

Special acknowledgement is due to those who made the research materially possible: the Department of French, University College Dublin, for granting a term's sabbatical leave in spring 1997; and the Ireland Fund of France, whose generous award, arranged through the good offices of its late Vice-Chairman Ambassador Tadhg F. O'Sullivan, greatly helped the promotion of the book.

Mr Donal Kelly, former cultural attaché at the Irish Embassy in Paris, first suggested that I ought to consider making a book out of the Saint-Lô story; Anna and Tony Farmar reacted to the project with immediate interest, and have been generous in taking on the risky business of publishing it. For his helpful comments on the typescript I am indebted to Barry McGovern, and for reading and editing my French summary, to Sylvie Kleinman-Batt.

Finally, for putting up with my obsession and for providing editorial advice and moral support, I thank my immediate family: my husband, Cormac Ó Cuilleanáin, daughters, Léan and Órla Ní Chuilleanáin and son, Eoin Ó Cuilleanáin.

Inevitably, there will be others whose memories of the hospital are not included in this book. To those, whom I have been unsuccessful in tracing, I apologise, and hope that this account at least records something of their experience of bringing aid to Normandy over fifty years ago.

Phyllis Gaffney
Dublin 1999

1: Saint-Lô 1944, *capitale des ruines*

> 'One may thus be excused if one questions the opinion generally received, that ten years will be sufficient for the total reconstruction of Saint-Lô.'
>
> *Samuel Beckett*

On the evening of D-Day, 6 June 1944, Allied bombers began a series of raids on the little Normandy town of Saint-Lô, then in German hands. Capital of the Département de la Manche, that region of Normandy that juts out into the English Channel, Saint-Lô lies directly on the route from the Normandy beaches to the heart of France. At that time the thriving market town had a population of around 11,700. Its strategic position, at the base of the Cotentin peninsula at a nexus of important routes to the Normandy beaches, made it one of the Allies' main targets. As long as the Germans held Saint-Lô the invading forces were bottled up in Normandy. Night after night, for the best part of a week, bombers relentlessly droned over the town, dropping their lethal cargo as comprehensively as possible. What the bombs failed to destroy was consumed by fire. Hundreds of civilians were killed and Saint-Lô was transformed into a heap of charred and ruined buildings, acquiring the unenviable distinction of being the most heavily destroyed town in France, with nine out of ten of its buildings reduced to rubble.

Just before the attack was launched, the Allies had dropped leaflets over the towns designated for bombing with warning messages, urging civilians to leave at once and take refuge in the countryside. Sadly, the messages never fell on Saint-Lô,

Healing amid the ruins

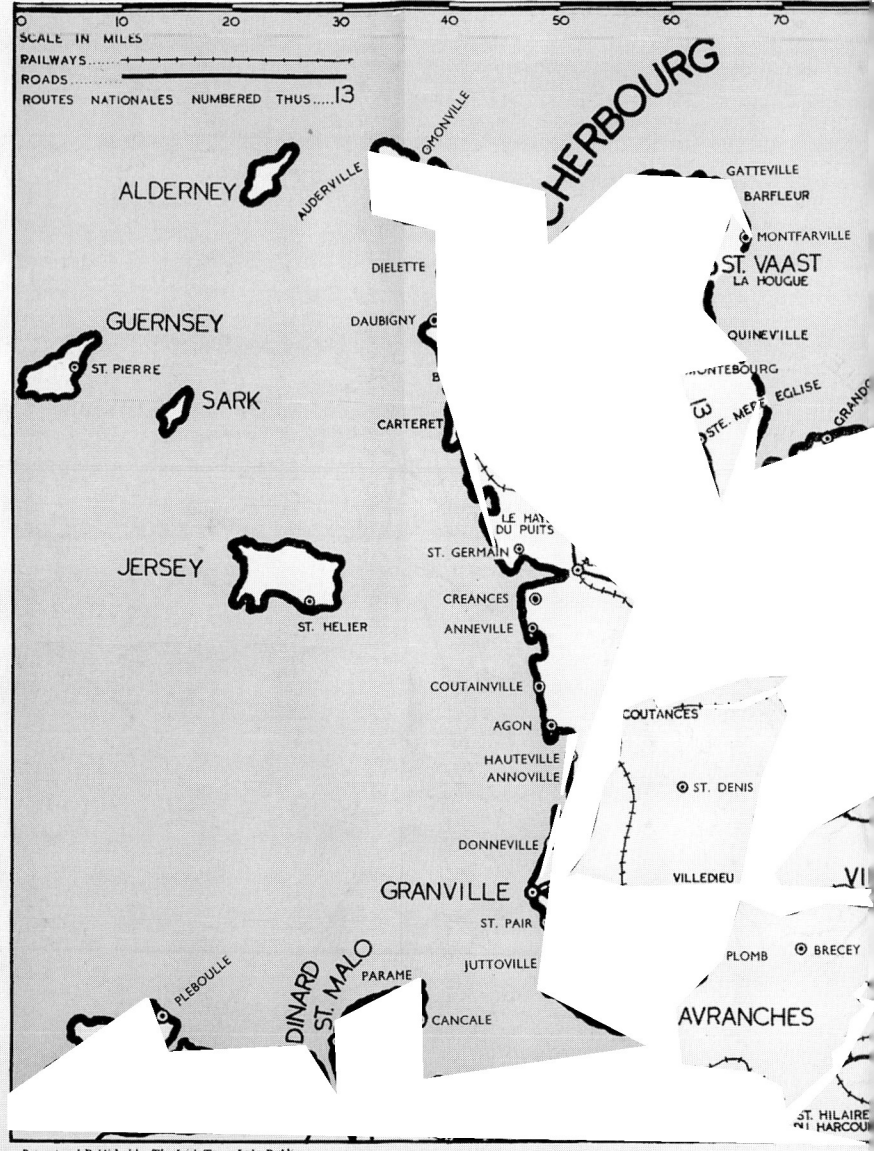

Saint-Lô 1944, capitale des ruins

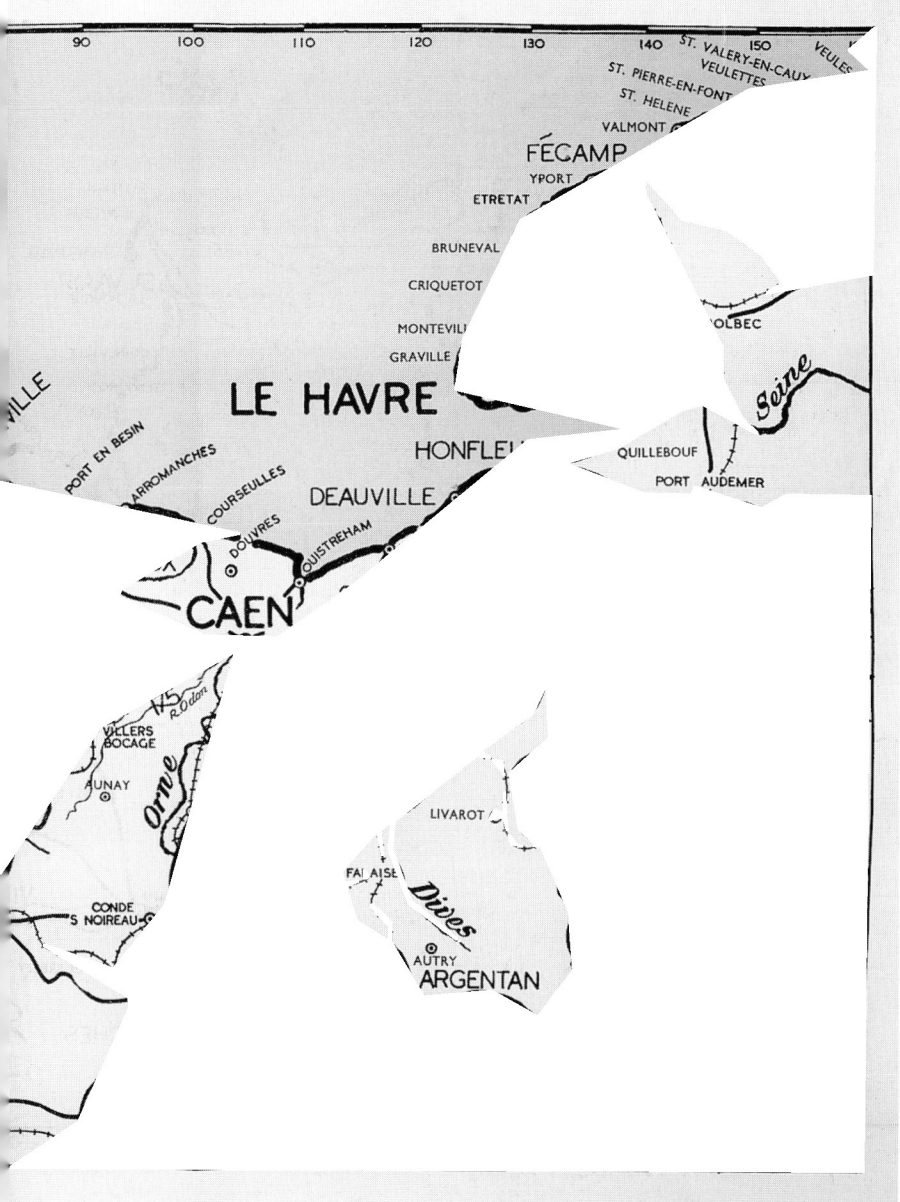

Reproduced by permission of The Irish Times

but were blown eastwards by the wind. The warnings had little effect elsewhere: the leaflets did not name the towns to be evacuated, and moreover, the Germans had ordered civilians to obey the usual curfew and to stay at home, expressly forbidding any evacuation of the towns.

From the Allies' point of view, the priority was to delay the progress of German tanks in their advance towards the beaches where the Normandy landings were taking place. This was essential for the successful movement of the Allied troops deployed on the ground, who were greatly outnumbered. The strategy succeeded in part, as the air raids did hamper the German advance by forcing them to move their troops at night—and June nights are short. But, once the Allies had landed, the Germans, well dug into the hedgerows, put up a tenacious resistance. The Allies finally took Saint-Lô from the Germans towards the end of July, and it was from Saint-Lô that General Patton launched his offensive on German-occupied Brittany and further towards the Loire valley. By this time, the old town had been all but destroyed.

Originally known by the Gaulish name *Briovère* (meaning 'bridge over the river Vire'), Saint-Lô owes its name to Laudo, or Lô, a 6th-century bishop. The town's Gaulish name reflects its strategic position, as does its history. Saint-Lô was the target of Viking invasions in the 9th century; King Philip Augustus took it in 1203 during his reconquest of the region. It was sacked in 1346 by King Edward III's troops and occupied by the English for some three decades of the 15th century, to be liberated by Charles VII in 1449. Its Calvinist sympathies and proximity to the English Channel made it suspect in the eyes of the French Crown during the 16th-century religious wars, and its late Gothic church of Notre-Dame, a casualty of the bombs in 1944, had been vandalised on other occasions in its past, by Huguenots and Jacobites alike.

Such a litany of siege and counter-siege is typical of the history of many towns. Indeed, up to 1944, Saint-Lô's history reflects much of the history of Normandy, and even the history of France. A provincial French town *par excellence*, it boasts, like many another, its Gallo-Roman and Merovingian artefacts, its Sainte-Croix abbey and its Carolingian castle, and it can claim a handful of individuals of minor historical significance. Supporting the French Revolution at a crucial moment, it became the capital of the Manche Department in 1795, leading to a period of economic and demographic growth during the 19th century.

France's participation in the Second World War started on 3 September 1939 when, in alliance with Britain, it declared war against Germany. A so-called 'phoney war' lasted for nine months, ending with a lightning invasion by German forces and the fall of France. The country was divided into two zones: the '*État Français*' ruled from Vichy in the south and the German-occupied territory north of the Loire. The Germans arrived in Saint-Lô, as elsewhere in the occupied zone, in June 1940.

Although Saint-Lô had to endure hard times under German occupation, and had its share of Resistance activists and patriots, it did not suffer any more than hundreds of other small French towns. The relative ordinariness of its experience, however, was transformed on the evening of D-Day.

Contemporary accounts all concur in the profound disbelief and shock produced by the sound of planes overhead. A bomb had hit the railway station during the afternoon leading the inhabitants to believe that there would be no more bombs on Saint-Lô, since the communications network had already been targeted. Families were settling down to their evening meal when the second attack came. Many, lingering to enjoy the last hours of sunlight, were dining later than usual; their meals were rudely interrupted by the first of the night-time bombing raids, at about 8 p.m. One family, on returning to their ruined home in September, found the peas from that June supper still in the pot on the stove . . .

Just under one thousand civilians were killed in the Saint-Lô bombing and its aftermath. Many were buried alive, including seventy-six Resistance prisoners who died when the prison was hit during the night of 6–7 June. The old prison gate remains standing, as a kind of secular shrine to their patriotism.

Saint-Lô was by no means the only town in Normandy to be targeted by the Allies: in the Manche region alone, an estimated 617 communes out of 648 were either partially or totally destroyed, and out of a population of 438,000, 187,000 lost their homes. In terms of fatalities, Saint-Lô did not suffer more than other towns: the bombing of Caen, for example, caused the death of some 2,000 people, while in Saint-Lô less than half that figure lost their lives. But it was because the scale of the destruction at Saint-Lô was measured at over ninety per cent of its buildings that the Manche capital became known as the *capitale des ruines*, the 'capital of the ruins'.

The civilians who stayed in Saint-Lô made their way to the cellars of houses or to makeshift shelters, or to a large hollow space under the medieval ramparts, known as the 'tunnel'. This underground dugout, just a few yards from the main municipal hospital, had been excavated by the Germans the previous year. Complete with communicating corridors and separate rooms, the space was earmarked for use as an emergency hospital centre in the event of fighting in or around the town. This plan was implemented in June 1944. For the first three days of the Allied bombing, a few hundred people took refuge in this shelter, including patients evacuated from the nearby hospital. The dugout saved the lives of German soldiers and French civilians alike, and even sheltered some wounded American prisoners, since it functioned as a kind of makeshift hospital. Emergency medical aid was also provided for the injured at the nearby Bon Sauveur psychiatric hospital, where some women gave birth and some of the wounded were treated. But this small clinic's resources were soon overstretched and, when its turn came to be hit on Thursday 8 June, three of its nursing sisters and two patients were killed.

Despite the heroic efforts of medical personnel in the town, all of those seriously injured died. In some cases, their lives could have been saved, had there been adequate rescue and surgical services. To make matters worse, during the course of the night of 6 June the main municipal hospital and the six pharmacies of Saint-Lô were all destroyed.

Over the remaining days of the first week, the more able-bodied in the town set about rescuing people trapped beneath crumbling masonry, and identifying and burying those who had lost their lives. Survivors have vivid memories of the sights, sounds and smells of that infernal week when Saint-Lô burned. Bombs still fell in rapid succession, with no warning sirens as the local electricity power station had been sabotaged by resistance activists. People were choked with plaster dust and fumes from burning buildings. Visibility was minimal in the smoke; and everywhere there was a ghastly smell of sulphur and burnt flesh.

The initial Allied plan was to take the town on 15 June, or D-Day + 9. The combined effect of the German counter-offensive, bad weather conditions and a terrain that was easier to defend than to attack, made this impossible.

When it became clear that the bombing raids were going to continue, hordes of inhabitants began to make their way out of the town. Believing or hoping that liberation was imminent, they made for farmsteads close to the outskirts. As the weeks of bombing and fighting went on, and as the air attacks were replaced by artillery fire, small communities of refugees formed in farms and villages close by. Some who had been traumatised by collapsing buildings preferred to sleep in ditches, hedgerows or orchards. Although food was available on the farms, with reasonably plentiful supplies of milk, eggs, vegetables, cider and calvados (frequently used as a disinfectant), rations had to be organised, given the multitudes of people to be

Healing amid the ruins

fed. Finding flour for baking bread was a daily struggle, particularly as it was often requisitioned by German officers. Ad hoc medical centres were set up in granaries, stables and living-rooms. Houses were turned into clinics. The commune of Le Hutrel, in particular, which received a large number of evacuees, functioned as a temporary hospital. Rudimentary operations were carried out; some died; some were born. One doctor performed amputations with a butcher's saw. And all the time, the battle raged around the area, as the refugees lived from day to day in persistent uncertainty as to the direction the war was taking.

Although access to the ruined town was barred by the German army still defending it, some evacuees managed to get past the guards to recover precious personal belongings, money or food. Others simply wanted to see what, if anything, was left of their homes. During these forays, wheelbarrows, prams and suitcases were loaded and brought back to the farms where people were camping.

During these catastrophic weeks of June and July 1944, the administrative forms of French civilian life were preserved to a remarkable extent by local mayors and officials, who held emergency meetings more or less daily in the different centres of evacuation, often interrupted by bombing or artillery fire. They were thus able to ensure that evacuees had sufficient food and shelter, that the injured and ill were looked after, and, as they made it their business to draw up lists of refugees, they played a significant role in helping people to locate missing friends or relatives. They issued *certificats de sinistrés* (survivor certificates) which were the only identity papers that many now possessed. Furthermore, they were in a position to promise future compensation to farmers for the costs involved in supplying food to the crowds of homeless camped on their properties. In the midst of the chaotic conditions all around, administrative and financial orthodoxy was thus preserved.

Things took a new turn after a month of conflict. On 8

Saint-Lô 1944, capitale des ruins

July, the Germans ordered a general civilian evacuation of the area around Saint-Lô, under pain of summary execution. This command may have been designed to prevent Franco-Allied collusion, or perhaps simply to minimise civilian casualties. So a further mass exodus took place, under the supervision of German soldiers. People headed in all directions, radiating further south, north, west and east of the immediate battle zone. Again, refugees were received and put up in farms, villages and communes further afield.

The nightmarish experiences of the town's inhabitants have been recorded in various eyewitness accounts. Two separate memories, of papers scattered in fields and blown by the wind, stand out as an image of the futility of war: the Allies' warning leaflets which most Saint-Lô people never saw, because they had been blown away from the town; and the hallucinatory experience, during the exodus from Saint-Lô, of walking through a field and finding it strewn with sheets of paper of different sizes and shapes, some torn and charred, some intact. The provenance of these documents was soon clear: the town archives had been bombed, and here was the entire store of municipal, regional and legal records literally scattered like autumn leaves to the four winds. The loss of public records was irreparable for historians, lawyers and administrators, as many of them had not yet been explored or even catalogued.

Saint-Lô finally fell to the Allies on 25 July, after seven weeks of battle. In the conflict, Allied troops sustained enormous casualties. One estimate sets at 11,000 the number of North American soldiers killed during the protracted battles, a toll almost equal to the town's whole population. To cater for casualties the Americans set up a huge (1,500-bed) temporary hospital near Cherbourg, about thirteen miles from Omaha beach.

The US Army at first banned civilians from returning to Saint-Lô, as dangers lurked in the charred ruins: unexploded bombs and mines still lay hidden under the rubble, shaky masonry was liable to fall with no warning, craters were camouflaged by fallen debris, and there was the grave risk of infection from corpses and stagnant waters. Residents returned to the heap of ruins that had been their home town, to be greeted by the Americans who had secured the victory. One family returning to find their home in ruins, heard a tiny miaow, and were met by their cat, which had turned wild after living through the ordeal of the previous two months. American GIs in trucks filed through the roadways which had been cleared of rubble, and threw sweets to the inhabitants. A handful of families who had remained in cellars during the weeks of fighting responded by throwing flowers, and produced bottles of wine which they had hidden away for this great day.

The immediate aftermath of summer 1944 has been documented in detail by Auguste-Louis Lefrançois, a pharmacist from Saint-Lô. It is a story of the gradual restoration of normality, when civilian life struggled back to its feet again, against all the odds, through the sheer will of the people. France remained at war with Germany until 8 May 1945, and even well after hostilities ceased daily life was characterised by improvisation and mutual assistance.

In the beginning, therefore, only those involved in the work of clearing up were allowed to live in the town. Commercial life was reborn by the end of August 1944, when nearby farmers set up stalls among the ruins to sell fruit, vegetables and dairy products. Bakers began to bake again, using flour provided by the Americans.

However, the very survival of Saint-Lô as a town and a departmental capital was in question. The municipal and regional administration, including the *préfecture*, or police headquarters, were transferred to the nearby town of Coutances. It was suggested, by outsiders, that to rebuild Saint-Lô would be pointless. One Allied major, in horror at the sight of the devastated town, thought that 'the deep sepulchral craters should be preserved as a supreme warning to posterity, as a monument to the havoc wrought by war'. But such opinions were not well

Saint-Lô 1944, capitale des ruins

received by the inhabitants.

An ad hoc municipal administration was appointed, without elections, as there was neither a postal service nor an electoral register in place, and since in any case the whereabouts of all the town's evacuees was not known. Meeting first on 11 October 1944, this body was presided over by Georges Lavalley, who subsequently served as mayor of the town. It organised a liberation ceremony that month and the population thronged the ruins to demonstrate their determination to see their administrative capital live again. Many in the crowd had felt snubbed by de Gaulle's visit to the Manche region in September, when he had been officially received in Coutances, and had completely bypassed Saint-Lô.

November 1944 brought some reassurance: the *Ministre de la Reconstruction et de l'Urbanisme* (Minister for Reconstruction and Town Planning) appointed André Hilt as the architect responsible for the rebuilding of the town. This was a popular decision, as Hilt was well liked and had a reputation for hard work. Perhaps more importantly, his appointment meant that the authorities in Paris believed the town did have a future. Yet doubts remained. Lefrançois, for instance, recorded the prevailing unease about the fate of Saint-Lô, combined with distrust of outsiders from central government*: 'nous eûmes assez souvent l'impression que le sort de Saint-Lô restait en suspens'* (we quite often had the impression that the fate of Saint-Lô was hanging in the balance). Such fears were not allayed when de Gaulle's Minister for Reconstruction, Raoul Dautry, on a visit to Saint-Lô in the spring of 1945, expressed the view that the town should be reconstructed at a new site near the neighbouring village of Lison. However, on a return visit to the region during the anniversary of the Normandy campaign, on 10 June 1945, de Gaulle made a memorable speech in Saint-Lô about its *ruines incomparables* and ended by exclaiming, to tumultuous applause: '*Vive Saint-Lô, chef-lieu du département de la Manche!*—in effect, making a promise that the *préfecture*

Healing amid the ruins

would be restored to its rightful home as soon as possible.

The interim council's first priority, apart from starting to clear the rubble and find and bury the dead, was to re-install the supply of drinking water, at first by carrying it in barrels from the countryside. Reconnecting the electricity network, draining the stagnant muddy pools which filled the bomb craters, and restoring some kind of rudimentary system for collecting household rubbish, were among the other Herculean tasks to be achieved. Full restoration of the town's electric light was only completed by March 1945. In the meantime, some people managed to light up the dark evenings by improvising oil-lamps in the skins of baked potatoes.

The wet winter of 1944–5 made conditions even more wretched for those living in the ruins. Some civilians were housed a little better in German military huts, which the Americans had initially wanted to burn as enemy installations. Rain penetrated everywhere, soon giving rise to ubiquitous mud.

Hordes of rats roamed the town, especially in the municipal cemetery, where some tombs had been dislocated by the bombing. There was no rat-poison, as the only source, in Paris, was barred to civilians by American military police.

For the first few months, this Beckettian streetscape of mud, rats and ruins was psychologically isolated from the rest of France. During the occupation, to combat resistance activity, the Germans had confiscated all the radio sets in the town, and these had been burned in the bombing of the Hôtel de Ville on 6 June. Communication with the outside world was restored, however, when a telephone exchange was installed before Christmas, on 17 December 1944, and when, as a New Year present in January 1945, the *Radiodiffusion française* offered the town two radio apparatuses with public address systems. The townspeople were particularly pleased that the official time of day was now verifiable. Two sirens used to wail through the ruins three times a day, so that everyone knew when it was eight in the morning, midday and six in the evening.

Saint-Lô 1944, capitale des ruins

Before the bombing, church bells had tolled the Angelus twice a day.

Those trying to live in the ruined town faced appalling health hazards, recorded in a contemporary account: 'The inhabitants of the ghost town live under broken walls or in cellars. The cellars have to be emptied with buckets several times a night. . . . As the water is of highly dubious quality, a typhoid epidemic is latent; as there is no soap, scabies is rampant; as mud and water penetrate everywhere, illness is rife . . . It's pretty well disaster personified.'

One of the most glaring immediate needs was for an adequate medical service. The main municipal hospital which, as we have seen, was destroyed by the Allied bombing, had provided five hundred beds and had enjoyed a good reputation. Its shell remained standing beside the river Vire, but it became a breeding-ground for rats and was to be demolished in 1947. The psychiatric hospital, the Bon Sauveur, had likewise been destroyed, with the exception of one stone structure. A small fifty-bed hospital, called the *hôpital Saint-Joseph Sainte-Geneviève*, was reinstated in this building after the war, and run by a religious order of nursing sisters and local doctors, including Dr Verrières, the surgeon, Dr Lecouillard in medicine and Dr Jean Bourdon, who cared for tubercular patients. Their efforts, although admirable, could not fully meet the needs of the town.

Some sick people went to Coutances or Bayeux for treatment; others relied on local doctors in or around Saint-Lô, including Dr Albert Philippe, a Resistance prisoner who had survived the bombing of the prison in June. They did what they could to alleviate illness. Trojan work was carried out in very difficult conditions but the shortage of rudimentary health requirements, particularly pharmaceuticals, was a serious problem. All the pharmacies of the town had been bombed, and all but one of them had also burned after the bombing. There was one pharmacy in Coutances and another in Carentan. This meant, in practice, a journey of fifty kilometres for an aspirin or a bandage.

The chronicler of this period, Auguste-Louis Lefrançois, set up an interim pharmacy with a colleague. They managed to procure a single trunk full of supplies from an English source, but were cut off by the continuing war from their normal suppliers in the Paris region. A building was found, but its roof had to be repaired. When slates were collected from the ruins, carried on peoples' backs, they had to wait for over a month to borrow the only remaining ladder in the town. Lefrançois was given a counter by a retired pharmacist in the region, pigeon-holes for storing stocks were improvised out of ammunition boxes, and some supplies were salvaged from the one pharmacy of the town that had not been completely burned. The shortage of pharmaceutical supplies lasted until February 1945, when a batch from Paris, ordered the previous October, was finally delivered.

Then in April 1945 news of help came from an unexpected quarter: the Irish Red Cross was to set up a hospital in the north of France and Saint-Lô had been chosen as the site for this project. The offer was welcomed with enthusiasm. But how had it come to be made?

2: The Irish Red Cross hospital unit

'the Irish bringing gifts'

Samuel Beckett

The Irish Red Cross Society had been planning since 1943 to send medical help to civilian casualties of the war in Europe. Established in July 1939, with close links with the Irish Army Medical Service, the society was very active during the Emergency (as the Second World War was somewhat ludicrously styled in neutral Southern Ireland). Its responsibilities included organising, with local government, local defence against the threat of invasion, whether from the Allied or the Axis powers, and the relief of distress at home and abroad. Its emergency hospitals supply depot at 15 Lincoln Place, Dublin, opened in January 1940 and ran throughout the war, with about one hundred and fifty sub-depots around the country; its volunteers manufactured bandages, dressings and wound pads; it maintained a fleet of almost ninety ambulances, ran a blood donation centre, and began an anti-tuberculosis campaign in January 1943.

The society made grants totalling £240,000 to famine-stricken India and to war victims and refugees in various European countries and sent parcels to prisoners of war and wounded soldiers abroad. At one stage, during the heaviest air raids in Britain, its reception centre for refugees at Dún Laoghaire pier welcomed an estimated one thousand arrivals a day. By mid-1945, it had 700 branches with 45,000 members, over half of whom had undergone medical or ancillary training. At the end of the war, 'Operation Shamrock' organised the temporary accommodation in Ireland of hundreds of children from France and Germany.

Funding for all these activities (and for the Irish hospital in Saint-Lô) was raised during the war by two principal methods, voluntary donations which totalled £152,000 by September 1945, and the holding of sweepstakes which raised some £184,000. The continued funding of the hospital in Saint-Lô was later to become an issue, as we shall see.

The first plan for medical aid to Europe took the form of a one-hundred-bed mobile hospital unit, fully self-sufficient and capable of operating anywhere it might be needed. Over a series of meetings in summer 1943 the Irish Red Cross drew up detailed specifications for this hugely ambitious project; the list of equipment covers eight foolscap pages. The plan proved unworkable, however, both because the Irish Army could not spare the required medical personnel, and because the secretary of the Department of External Affairs believed the British to be hostile to the whole idea. He wrote to the Department of the Taoiseach: 'I enclose a copy of Lord Cranbourne's letter . . . You will see through the webs of politeness that they don't want our unit. What they do want is that our doctors should join British Units as individuals.' Lord Cranbourne's letter pointed out that plans for the future administration of liberated European territory remained uncertain—he was writing in September 1943, nine months before the Normandy landings—and that when the time came, the first call would be made on Britain's own voluntary societies.

After the Allied invasion in June 1944 the society made direct overtures to the French regarding its mobile hospital project. On 24 August—the eve of the liberation of Paris—Martin McNamara, the society's secretary, wrote to his counterpart at the emergency committee of the French Red Cross, then temporarily stationed in London, offering to send a medical unit to France, with or without individual doctors 'in Irish Red Cross uniform or in civilian dress, and also to send such supplies of medical and surgical equipment' as could be obtained.

Enthusiastic letters arrived from the French Red Cross's president, General Adolphe Sicé, and its secretary, Georges Mathieu. General Sicé declared himself touched by the Irish proposal, which he was submitting to both the provisional government of France and the Allied high command. Mathieu talked of travelling to Dublin and following his visit a fortnight later, in mid-September, the society's original plan to send an ambulance unit to Europe had crystallised into an agreement to send a hospital unit to France, with the precise location still to be designated.

Diplomatic relations between France and Ireland were rather delicate during this period. At the very time when the Irish Red Cross was making overtures to the French, de Gaulle's provisional government was demanding the replacement of all heads of mission from neutral countries who had served in Vichy. The Irish government insisted that an exception be made for its representative, Seán Murphy, who had been Ireland's minister in France since December 1938. The new French administration eventually yielded to the Irish request, and agreed in early October 1944 that Murphy could remain as Ireland's envoy accredited to France.

However, the question of whether or not Murphy would be required to present new letters of credence was discussed in a substantial amount of diplomatic correspondence between Dublin and Paris, and Paris and London. Many factors were weighed up in the debate, not least the matter of Ireland's constitutional position in relation to Britain. In the meantime, Murphy, having no credentials to present, and thus being unable to pay a courtesy visit to de Gaulle, returned to Dublin from December 1944 to March 1945, in order to facilitate a resolution. The whole matter, not helped by communications difficulties, was only concluded in the spring, when General de Gaulle finally received Mr Murphy in a private audience on

24 March 1945; and the French also dropped their insistence on new letters of credence, making a considerable concession towards Ireland.

There is some evidence in French diplomatic papers that the Irish Red Cross's offer of a hospital played a role in promoting this concession. The hospital offer was interpreted by French diplomats as a symptom of a shift in Irish foreign policy towards continental Europe. A telegram to the Quai d'Orsay dated 15 September 1944, for example, sent by France's ambassador in Dublin, Xavier de Laforcade, spells out the political dimension of the Irish Red Cross's humanitarian gesture: *'Je n'hésite donc pas à voir là un geste politique; le plus significatif que l'on puisse concevoir dans le cadre et à la limite de la neutralité à laquelle le Gouvernement irlandais reste attaché. Ce dernier désire évidemment resserrer les liens qui unissent les deux peuples et, d'une façon plus générale, multiplier ses rapports directs avec les pays du continent européen dont la France est le plus proche.'* ('I therefore have no hesitation in viewing this as a political gesture; the most significant one imaginable, within the framework and the boundaries of the neutral stance that the Irish Government persists in maintaining. That government is obviously intent on strengthening the ties that link our two peoples and, more generally, on increasing Ireland's direct links with the countries of Continental Europe, France being the closest.') Moreover, it was noted, such a rapprochement between Ireland and France was ultimately in France's own best interests: the more that small nations turned towards France, the greater was the possibility of counterbalancing what was seen as increasing Anglo-American influence on the world stage.

Given the strained state of Franco-Irish diplomatic relations for a period of about six months, it is all the more remarkable that the Irish hospital project proceeded as smoothly as it did. Negotiations with the French authorities were fraught with other difficulties. Not only was communication hindered by the continuing war, but following the liberation of Paris on 25

The Irish Red Cross hospital unit

August 1944 it was not at all clear who was exercising power. Tensions existed between the French, jealous of their newly regained sovereignty, and their allies, for whom French territory was still part of the war zone, and who did not formally recognise the legitimacy of de Gaulle's provisional government until 23 October 1944, some two months after the fall of the Vichy régime. De Gaulle's own authority was by no means assured, especially in the south-west, where other forces, such as communists, vied with Gaullists for local control. On the Allied side, military leaders did not always co-operate or consult with their diplomatic colleagues, whom at times they chose to ignore.

The hospital scheme went public in Ireland with the *Irish Press* announcing Mathieu's visit to Dublin, on behalf of the French Red Cross, on 14 September 1944. On 24 September, in the 'Red Cross Half-Hour' broadcast—a regular Sunday evening slot on Radio Éireann in summer 1944—the chairman, Conor Maguire, referred to a similar event of over seventy years before: 'In the month of August, 1871, there arrived in Dublin a remarkable delegation. It was led by Count de Flavigny, President of the French Society for the Relief of the Wounded . . . The Delegation had been sent to Ireland by the French Red Cross to thank the Irish people for sending a fully staffed and equipped Ambulance Unit to France during the war of 1870.'

History was now repeating itself, and this time the Irish aid was to 'take the form of a one-hundred bed Hospital to serve the civilian population in an area to be chosen by the Irish Red Cross Society in consultation with the French Red Cross Society. . . . In certain towns where heavy fighting had taken place hospital services for the civilian population are reduced to one-fourth, and in some areas are practically non-existent.'

Staff recruitment was launched by advertisements in the Irish daily newspapers on 1 October, 1944, while Allied and French troops were pressing eastwards towards the German border in the final stages of the war. The advertisements made it clear that conditions would be primitive, but the levels of pay being offered were reasonable. The response was encouraging. By 23 October, the closing date, over three times the number of doctors required had offered their services, and over six hundred letters expressing interest in the venture had arrived at 21 St Stephen's Green, the society's headquarters, from all parts of the country and from all levels of staff. No doubt many of the applicants were motivated by a sense of adventure as well as altruism, and a desire to be involved directly in world events after years on the sidelines.

By the end of December 1944 about fifteen doctors as well as some clerical and technical staff had been appointed. One of the first physicians to be recruited was Alan Thompson who had graduated with an MB from Trinity College in 1930 and became consultant to the Richmond, Rotunda and Whitworth hospitals in Dublin. He and his brother, Geoffrey, who was a psychiatrist, were close friends of Samuel Beckett whom Alan was later to recruit for the Saint-Lô project. The two brothers and Beckett had been at school together in Portora Royal School in Enniskillen.

Mary Crowley, who had been assistant matron of the Royal Victoria Eye and Ear Hospital in Dublin, was appointed matron to the Saint-Lô hospital in December 1944 and served on the selection committee for recruiting nursing staff. Seventy-one Irish-trained nurses were interviewed over four days in January 1945, with a view to selecting thirty to thirty-five out of over two hundred applicants.

Securing the medical director identified as essential to the project was more difficult. The society was determined that Colonel Thomas McKinney, the director of the army medical services and member of the society's central council since its foundation, should direct the hospital in France. Born in 1887, McKinney was a man of wide organisational experience. He spoke French, German, Irish and Spanish and had taken a consignment of Red Cross aid to Spain in 1943. In spite of previous rebuffs from the Minister for the Co-ordination of Defensive Measures, who maintained that army officers could not be spared during the Emergency, the society persisted in the pursuit of its man. Eventually, in the autumn of 1944, McKinney was released from the army on secondment, with the Red Cross looking after his salary, insurance and pensions.

Thus, by January 1945 most of the staff had been recruited. But since the assembly of equipment and supplies which were to be sent with the personnel was only just beginning, and the site of the hospital had not yet been chosen, the recruits had a long and frustrating wait before embarking for France.

In the meantime, the 'colossal task'—in the words of the matron, Mary Crowley—of transporting 'a complete hospital from one country to another and [setting] in motion every department fully equipped and staffed' was begun. A special French hospital unit equipment and co-ordinating subcommittee of the Irish Red Cross Society held regular meetings, to plan the acquisition of items ranging from bandages and penicillin to spare parts for cookers, wheels for trolleys, electric bulbs and telephone wiring. Some domestic supplies, such as four crates of enamel kitchen-ware and one ton of jam and marmalade, were donated, but most were bought, with a grant of £1,200 from the executive committee in December 1944.

Those medical supplies obtainable in Ireland were partly acquired through the Department of Defence; other supplies, harder to come by, were obtained through the American Red Cross or British sources. Voluntary Red Cross workers gathered the medical supplies and made clothing, bedlinen and dressings. This work of assembling, sewing and packing took place at the emergency depot in Lincoln Place, Dublin, which became a hive of industry in the spring of 1945. Mary Crowley recalled her efforts in overseeing the task, which she undertook with two colleagues:

'With the help of Mrs Hackett and Mrs Fahy, I was able to

prepare a list of the fundamental requirements of a hospital of 100 beds, plus 60 staff, for example—beds, tables, chairs, screens, linen, bedding, clothing, cookery, cooking utensils, stores, refrigerators, fuel, medical appliances, toilet requirements, dressing, drugs, food, etc., and as a team we assembled all the requirements in Lincoln Place.' Then there was the securing of thousands of specialised items, 'many of which were only obtained under great difficulty, but were indispensable, the least of which might have put out of action a whole department if not available.'

On 28 March 1945, a delegation from the Irish Red Cross travelled to Paris to negotiate with the French authorities and to choose the site for the proposed Irish hospital. The four members of the group were Colonel McKinney, Commandant C. J. Daly, in charge of supplies, Dr Alan Thompson, and Michael Scott, the prominent Dublin architect. Scott, then aged thirty-nine, had some experience in hospital design and had been asked to act as architectural adviser to the Irish Red Cross. In Paris the group met personnel from the French Red Cross and de Gaulle's Minister for Public Health, before being driven to Brittany and Normandy in the company of M. le Comte d'Allières, foreign relations officer of the central body of the French Red Cross. The French proposed two possible locations for the hospital: the port of Brest in Brittany which had been largely destroyed by fire—the option preferred by the Irish—and, further to the east, Saint-Lô.

Michael Scott remembered the Irish delegation's first arrival in Saint-Lô: 'When we got there, there was nothing at all. The whole of Saint-Lô was blotted out. Nothing was standing except a few little shacks that had been temporarily put up, and in one of these wooden shacks was the local hospital, a room of about twenty feet by twelve. One nurse kept explaining how it happened, the planes coming around and around, bombing Saint-Lô from a very considerable height. They were American planes.'

The Irish Red Cross hospital unit

Colonel McKinney visited Saint-Lô again in April, in the company of the Irish Minister, Seán Murphy, and the French Minister for Reconstruction, Raoul Dautry. On his return, in a radio broadcast on 17 May, he described the ghostly atmosphere in Brest which had been destroyed by fire:

'I arrived in Brest by road about 10 p.m. and didn't discover the city until I was actually in the ruins. There were no distant lights, no glow in the sky to indicate its proximity. And there was no official black-out. There was nothing to be seen in the city itself but rubble and gaunt walls. . . . It was as silent as a city of the dead. After a little, occasional glimmers of light were to be seen—some apparently high-up in the walls. Some of the inhabitants had returned to the ruins. I gathered that this is a feature of a town destroyed in France. In Saint-Lô— the scene of our prospective labours—which was destroyed by aerial bombardment, I was told that many of the former residents have returned to live in the cellars—though personally I got the impression that all the cellars must be choked with debris. After considerable delay and wandering through the narrowed streets of Brest we succeeded in discovering humanity and making the necessary contacts. Whilst daylight dissipated the eerie ghostly feeling associated with darkness in the ruins, the daylight scene confirmed the first feelings of depression. One of the main shelters in the city remains barred up— a mourning wreath attached to the gate. One thousand people lost their lives in that shelter. Daylight also showed that Brest was not completely destroyed. Saint-Lô, on the other hand, may be described as 100 per cent flattened—the work of a few hours from the air. War in passing had left a trail of ruin in the countryside. Wrecked and rusty tanks and guns dotting the road-side and adjacent fields, bomb-craters and ruined, isolated houses or villages, particularly at cross-roads, marked its path.'

McKinney concluded by appealing to the generosity of his compatriots: 'The world will expect the Irish Red Cross as representing a nation which had escaped the ravages and horrors of war to play a full part. Help—much help—will be needed.'

Saint-Lô, as the worst affected of France's bombed towns, was chosen for the Irish hospital of about one hundred beds. A French architect, M. Lafont, was preparing drawings of the hospital—a set of one-storey wooden huts with communicating passage-ways—and these were approved by Michael Scott. The buildings were to be provided by the French Ministry of Reconstruction, which would also be responsible for installing plumbing, sewage, electricity and heating, while the Irish Red Cross Society would supply the equipment and staff for an indefinite period.

Potential conflicts of interest were identified at the outset by Alan Thompson, who stated in his report to the central council of the Red Cross on his return from France that Irish personnel did not appear to be required either in Brest or Saint-Lô but that there was a very definite desire for the medical supplies. But he went on to inform the council that 'the authorities in Paris, however, appeared to favour the establishment of a complete Irish Unit consisting of personnel and equipment'.

The gathering of supplies for the hospital continued while some of those recruited had to withdraw because of changed circumstance. Three of the first doctors to leave for France were Arthur Darley, Jim Gaffney and Frederick McKee. Darley was the son of a musician, also named Arthur Darley, and, like his father, was an accomplished instrumentalist, playing the violin, piano and guitar. He had qualified in Trinity medical school in 1931, and had worked at the Richmond Hospital, Dublin and Portrane Asylum before setting sail to work on a Canadian Pacific liner in 1937. Fluent in French, as some of his schooldays had been spent at the Benedictine College in Douai, he was to be in charge of the tuberculosis unit and the outpatients department.

Jim Gaffney was a pathologist, and also—unusually for a

The Irish Red Cross hospital unit

Catholic at that time—a TCD graduate. Qualifying in 1934, he had done some postgraduate training in Huntingdon before working at Trinity's school of pathology with an attachment to Sir Patrick Dun's Hospital. He was to spend the year in Saint-Lô on leave of absence. Frederick McKee had graduated in 1939 from the Royal College of Surgeons in Ireland, and had been working in Belfast's Royal Victoria Hospital.

The most famous of the recruits, whose name continues to draw attention to Saint-Lô, was Samuel Beckett, winner of the Nobel Prize for Literature in 1969. He was a keen observer of the project, and his sharp, slightly alienated comments add nuances to the official and informal accounts. He was recruited as storekeeper and interpreter in Dublin in late May 1945. Then aged thirty-nine, he had spent the war in France, where he had lived on and off since his time at the École Normale Supérieure in Paris in 1928–30 and where he had made numerous close friends, including James Joyce. In early September 1939, the moment the war broke out, Beckett had deliberately cut short a visit to Ireland to return to the French capital—preferring, as he later remarked, 'France at war to Ireland at peace'. He initially intended to volunteer his services as an ambulance driver but, after the German invasion in 1940, joined the Resistance, until the cell he was attached to was betrayed and he had to flee from the Gestapo, with his companion, Suzanne Deschevaux-Dumesnil, into the relatively safer unoccupied French territory of the south. He had spent the last two years of the war with Suzanne, later to become his wife, in the Vaucluse village of Roussillon d'Apt, working as a farm labourer in return for food.

After the liberation, he went back to Dublin to visit his family, who had not seen him since 1939. He was anxious to return to France, but was encountering difficulties as a foreign national without a job. Alan Thompson suggested that Beckett apply for the post of quartermaster-storekeeper which the society was anxious to fill with 'if possible, a fluent French speaker' who could also act as interpreter. This solved Beckett's problem and he took up his storekeeping duties in Dublin in July, familiarising himself with some of the hospital cargo before it sailed. He had an extremely meticulous mind and a regard for detail which had already been put to good use while working for the Resistance, gathering information from various sources about enemy installations, classifying, typing and translating it, before passing it on to be microfilmed for British intelligence.

By the middle of July 1945, six ambulances, a utility wagon and a lorry, and other heavy equipment—such as two electrical generators and one fumigator—together with some two or three hundred tons of food and medical supplies, sealed and packed into approximately 3,500 packages, and with an estimated value of £30,000 to £40,000 (£800,000 in 1999 terms), were assembled and ready to sail to France. (The Dublin Port and Docks Board had placed a warehouse at the disposal of the Red Cross Society free of charge.) The cargo included 'all instruments necessary for a general operating theatre and for an extra theatre to deal with Gynaecological and Obstetrical cases. The complete food requirements of the Unit for six months, are being taken'. In addition, over 200 beds were being sent, for both patients and staff; and, besides the linen, surgical dressings, clothing, furniture and domestic equipment, all of which had been supplied by the emergency hospitals supplies committee, the consignment included quantities of whiskey and cigarettes as well as garden tools and seeds and furnishings for the chapel.

Colonel McKinney left for France on 4 August, followed three days later by Alan Thompson and Samuel Beckett and in late August by the three doctors, Gaffney, Darley and McKee, together with Michael Killick, laboratory technician, and Tommy Dunne, storeman.

Transport of the supplies was provided by the Wexford Steamship Company's vessel, the *Menapia*, which had been

The Irish Red Cross hospital unit

equipped with special cold storage facilities for penicillin and blood serum. On the eve of the ship's departure Jean Rivière, French Minister to Ireland, inspected the vessel and thanked the Irish Red Cross. The entire cargo was loaded at Alexandra Wharf and the ship set sail for Cherbourg on 14 August 1945. The hospital was at last on its way to France.

3: A hospital of wooden huts

'But I think that to the end of its hospital days it
will be called the Irish Hospital'
Samuel Beckett

'Saint-Lô is just a heap of rubble,' wrote Samuel Beckett soon after his arrival. 'It has been raining hard the last few days and the place is a sea of mud. What it will be like in winter is hard to imagine. No lodging of course of any kind.'

The advance party of McKinney, Thompson and Beckett stayed first in a local castle, at Canisy, owned by the Countess de Kergorlay, who was an active member of the French Red Cross. They then moved to the house of a local doctor, nearer to the hospital site, on the eastern edge of the town. The three men slept in one small room, with Beckett and Thompson sharing a bed. These conditions, and the delay in the hospital construction, evoked a stoical response from Beckett: 'The hospital buildings are far from ready, and there is no question of getting the place running properly before middle of November, if we ever get it running at all. . . . We are chivvying the architect to get at least one hut ready, even without water or sanitary arrangements, so that we can occupy it. The apparent apathy doesn't irritate me as it does the other two, whose reaction to the people is more or less the classical anglo-saxon exasperation. It is a tune of which I am tired.' The chivvying of the architect must have met with some success because when the next five members of the hospital staff arrived in Dieppe ten days later, one hut was ready.

One of the five, Jim Gaffney, described their arrival: 'we . . . were met by Col. McKinney and Sam Beckett (storekeeper).

A hospital of wooden huts

They had the big Ford V.8 Utility waggon with them . . . We weren't hungry as we had had an excellent four-course lunch on board and later tea; but nevertheless Sam brought us three huge bags of pears, grapes and plums. It was novel being driven on the right-hand side of the road and Sam believes in getting the 150 miles done as quickly as possible. . . . [he] is official interpreter as well as storekeeper and although a Dublin man has lived for ten years in France so the language is no trouble.'

Once in Saint-Lô 'it took us about three quarters of an hour to find the hospital. This wasn't surprising, as one street of ruins looks very much like another . . . there are acres of empty spaces, that is with rubble piled up 10–20 feet. Many of the streets can only be traversed on foot by stepping from one pile of bricks to another, or from one rusted girder on to the end of a buried bedstead. Many cellars still lie under the debris and demolition work goes on slowly but surely. Digging the other day, they found the body of one of the local bakers and two of his assistants; and as we arrived we heard the distant explosions of two mines, where they are clearing some mines in some fields. . . . We saw the Post Office which is gutted—you can see the sky through the empty windows and roof—it would have been about the size of Mountjoy Police Station. The Mental Hospital is also a shell, many of the inmates being killed. . . . For about six weeks the town kept changing hands between the Germans and the Americans. There are still about 5,000 people in it, but you would wonder where or how they live; mostly in boarded up cellars, on mattresses.'

The hospital site, between two roads leading out of the town, was wide and sloping. Before the war it had been divided into allotments for working people to grow vegetables. 'Just now,' wrote Gaffney, describing the state of progress at the end of August, 'there are ten white huts, quite large . . . made of wood lined à asbestos and bright with many windows and electric lighting; wooden uncarpeted floors; A.R.P. beds, each with a locker. Our clothes are thrown on a chair beside the bed or over one of the low-cross-ties under the ceiling. . . . the eight of us sleep, eat, write and read in this hut, which is the only complete one; the others are being wired or otherwise finished.' There was, as yet, no running water or proper sanitation.

The *Menapia* had arrived in Cherbourg on 20 August, met by McKinney, Thompson and Beckett who supervised the unloading of her cargo on to railway wagons, and thence to Saint-Lô. Having nothing much else to occupy them, the staff all participated in the job of fetching, unpacking and sorting out the crates, curious to see their contents. Jim Gaffney described the work:

'Dr. Thompson and Beckett and his assistant are superintending the stacking and sorting of the 250 tons of supplies. They are being brought from Cherbourg by rail and from there by lorry up here. "Here" means a store about half a mile from the hospital. This store consists of a badly-blitzed institution. It is a stud farm run by the State. They have about 400 horses on I don't know how many acres, and our store is in the lofts over the stables. They are huge, but are covered with bullet holes and not a window intact. Transport from station to store is done by lorry driven by German prisoners of war, who carry the heavy crates (1–4 cwt.) upstairs then to the lofts. They are fine hefty fellows and they would need to be; about 12–20 of them begin each day at 8 am superintended also by French guards with rifles.'

The Irish Red Cross hospital uniforms, which had been specially designed for the project, soon proved useless. August was one of the wettest months in Normandy for many years, and Gaffney longed for a good pair of dungarees like Beckett's, and for rubber boots for the muddy building site in which they were living. 'We go to the stores now and then to fetch items as we need them. For instance, we have all discarded our nice pansy uniform and have got into civilian suits; some of the workers like the storekeeper have dungaree-type uniform and if I had dungarees here I'd wear them. Outside the door is

A hospital of wooden huts

just clay and brick rubble and indeed all around. After two days rain it's just a wilderness of muck and wet; gum boots would then be ideal but I guess there's no way of getting them out. . . .

'This morning, and till about 5 p.m., we spent in the store shifting the stock and helping to sort out my stuff; and also to find a few extra items for our personal comfort.. . . [We] brought back some items to the "shack". These included one packing case about the size of the big wooden Pattersons match case, containing the items of recreation and books for the staff and patients. We dug out curious books, including some on Moral Theology; a dart board; a ring board; cards by Afton, Player and Gold Flake and Guinness and chess and draughts. It had also lots of thread (for the ladies, we presume).' Supplies included half a million cigarettes, too, donated in Ireland and packed in tins. Cigarettes were scarce in postwar France. Gaps in some of the supplies, including about sixty basic items out of a total of five hundred needed for the pathology laboratory, had somehow to be filled in France.

In September 1945, Gaffney described the slow progress with the hospital construction: 'the wood is scarce and so is everything else and it's too hot to work in the middle of the day', and expressed the staff's longing 'to see and hear running water again'. 'The workmen continue laying a road into the wilderness of huts, throwing stones on them, steamrolling them and going through a formality of concreting them. Then the sewer layers, the water main layers, the fitters, carpenters, electricians, bricklayers (for the 2-foot brick foundations) and painters—all are going from 7 a.m. till 7 p.m. Some work well, some dodge all the time.' The workers were French, Italian, Spanish, Algerian and German. 'The German POW camp here has about 1,000 men and they have their own POW doctor—a Dr Lippitt from Graz, Austria, who has written to his people 84 times without getting a reply. He speaks good English, often comes to tea and brings us the *Daily Mail* two days old. . .

Healing amid the ruins

.The German POW's like to work around the hospital as they get an odd cup of tea or cigarette extra. For example they clean our shoes, brush our clothes, etc.'

Improvisation was a recurring theme. Some US personnel from a prisoner of war camp nearby offered the Irish hospital 'armchairs and any amount of air strip material (in sections of steel grid three feet wide) to make iron paths around the hospital' as a form of protection from the ubiquitous mud on the ground. The distillation plant for the pathology laboratory was partly 'home-made', and the laboratory shelves were rigged up by recycling the timber and nails from the packing crates which had carried supplies from Ireland.

As the hospital was being constructed the town itself was slowly coming back to life. 'In the square near the Cathedral (which is quite demolished),' wrote Gaffney, 'there is a heap of rubble 30–40 feet high; the other day two men with two wheelbarrows began to remove it, God knows where.' Late in 1945 temporary accommodation for the residents was provided in the form of wooden huts, with provision for gas, electricity and running water, sent from various countries, including Sweden, Finland, Switzerland as well as North America and other regions of France.

New Irish staff arrived in small batches, mostly into Dieppe, during the months of September and October. So often were trips made to meet them that the hospital established a base for itself at the Hôtel des Arcades in the Norman port. The hotel was run by a homely couple who made the doctors and nurses feel very welcome. Beckett was usually the chauffeur, accompanied by another staff member. Thus, Beckett and Gaffney met George Stewart, the hospital carpenter and buildings supervisor, and Maurice Fitzgerald, transport supervisor, on 17 October. This pair brought a welcome packet from Dr Gaffney's family, including his dungarees.

Born in Paris, Fitzgerald's family had been marrying across the Franco-Irish divide for generations. He joined the French infantry, and managed to get out on the last British vessel to leave Saint Nazaire in 1940, just after Dunkirk. Making his way to Holyhead still clad in his French army uniform, he was closely interrogated at the Welsh port, but eventually allowed to take the mailboat to Dún Laoghaire. As Fitzgerald's grandfather had been born in Ireland, and as he was still under twenty-one, he was eligible to become an Irish citizen and went straight into the Irish Army.

His young wife, Meave, an active Red Cross volunteer, had intended to accompany her husband to Saint Lô—she had been recruited to work as a secretary at the hospital—but had to pull out through illness. In going to Saint-Lô Maurice was repeating a family tradition: his grandfather had been awarded Red Cross medals for service in France during the war of 1870–71.

Both Fitzgerald and Stewart were very good with their hands, and able to carry out all sorts of repair jobs. Stewart's services were in constant demand, in carpentry, plumbing and electrical work. Fitzgerald drove around in an ambulance, ferrying patients but also supplies of all sorts: he once transported a piano from a US base at Carentan.

Alan Thompson returned to Dublin in early October and was replaced as physician by Dr Desmond Leahy. A UCD graduate, Leahy had been attached to St Vincent's and Harcourt St Hospitals in Dublin, and had served with the army medical service in 1941 and 1942. He had been recruited in the early summer of 1945, having been approached by Dr Robert Collis, a committee member of the Irish Red Cross.

Leahy came through Paris, and missed the diplomatic representative who was to meet him at the Gare St Lazare. There was no answer from the Irish Embassy telephone number, so he spent his first night sleeping on a bunk in an American Red Cross dormitory. In the morning he contacted the embassy, and learned that he was supposed to be sharing a hotel room with Jim Gaffney. 'Sam Beckett was to drive us back to Saint-

Lô. He was staying in his own flat in Paris. On the journey we stopped for a short break. The only liquid available was a bottle of red wine. The problem of opening the bottle was solved by knocking the head off with a spanner.'

Meanwhile, the hospital had gradually begun to assume its healing function. An outpatients department was opened in early September and began to treat large numbers of patients with penicillin and other drugs. 'Penicillin was not available in Saint-Lô at this time,' Desmond Leahy recalls, 'and so its possession and use by the Irish Red Cross Hospital was an important event in the medical world of Saint-Lô and the surrounding area. The news spread that we had a wonder drug and some patients persuaded their doctor to send them to the Irish hospital hoping that the new drug might effect a cure. I remember a patient, crippled with rheumatoid arthritis, arriving on a stretcher, brought by ambulance by one of the relief organizations. We had to explain that penicillin could not effect a cure of that condition.'

One of the earliest outpatients to benefit from the hospital's penicillin was M. Marcel Menant, a former member of the provisional town council of 1944, who had been taken prisoner during the war and was suffering from boils on his knee. When he spoke to the present writer in 1997 M. Menant was in his nineties. He clearly recalled an experience, as an eight-year-old boy, during the Great War of 1914–18, when he climbed into wagons full of wounded soldiers on the instructions of his aunt, a Red Cross volunteer. He was small enough to clamber over the stretchers to carry bowls of broth and coffee to the wounded men. Three decades later, the Red Cross was recompensing his youthful good deed.

Gaffney referred to penicillin's black market price in Paris at the time: 'an ampoule of penicillin has been sold for £250; in Dublin its price is about 15s.' The Irish hospital ambulance drivers, whenever they had a consignment of this precious drug on board, were advised to carry a loaded pistol with them as a

A hospital of wooden huts

precaution against theft.

By early October the hospital's pathology laboratory was beginning to look as if it was in business. On the fourth Gaffney described his refrigerator, autoclave, incubator and water heater all in working order, and was looking forward to getting some bacteriology done. By the middle of the month, an x-ray plant had been installed, and a radiographer-nurse had been sent for. The laboratory was to cover pathology, bacteriology and biochemistry for the whole Manche region, and its facilities were offered to the medical profession in the area.

But relations with the local doctors were not straightforward. Soon after he arrived Beckett mentioned the unease of 'the local medical crowd'. He contrasts the 'stuff' which the Irish had brought with them—the supplies of penicillin and equipment which were very welcome—with the 'staff' who were perceived as a threat to the French doctors' livelihood: 'We have the impression that the locals would like the stuff, but don't want us (very reasonable attitude) and that the French Red Cross, for reasons not clear, insist on an Irish staff.'

Gaffney, too, mentions difficulties, writing in late August: 'The staff problem though is complex as there's no agreement yet between the local G.P.s as to what work we are to do (they want to provide the only surgeon for example) but they will need the services of a pathologist at any rate.' It appears that, in the short run at least, a working arrangement was reached. Gaffney writes, for example, in September 1945, that 'one evening last week we had a conference, informal, with the local doctors, four of them, to see just how we would work and what we'd do in regard to numbers of beds, etc. Briefly we modified our plan of operations.'

Local doctors availed of medicines dispensed by the hospital and Irish and French doctors maintained friendly social relations. Nonetheless, in early October, Gaffney wrote: 'The local medicos don't take kindly to us and this, we think, will be our principal obstacle. There's all sorts of activity going on behind the scenes, some of which only gets to our ken.'

That winter officials from the Ministry of Public Health, local health officials and representatives from the Irish hospital drew up a set of guidelines designed to integrate the hospital into the local health care system as well as to protect Saint-Lô doctors and pharmacists. Admissions to the Irish hospital were to be regulated; private patients and patients covered by insurance schemes were to be charged for treatment. Those entitled for economic reasons to free medical care, war veterans and occupational accident cases, as well as special cases designated by the mayor of the town as *sinistrés* (victims of the bombing) were to be completely free from charges and entitled to both treatment and medicines dispensed by the Irish. According to the guidelines, all inpatients, whether they be needy, insured, or private, were required to have a local doctor's certificate before being admitted. Such was the demand from the townspeople for medical care that these guidelines, which had given rise to some heated debates within the town council, were never strictly applied at the Irish hospital. Thus, the ground was laid for resentments which were to bubble to the surface the following summer and autumn.

In late autumn 1945 female staff began to arrive from Ireland. It was no accident that the installation of the first lavatory coincided with the arrival in October of the first of these, Clare Olden, from Cork, who was to work as secretary, and Marguerite Barrett, who was originally from Normandy and was to work as receptionist and sewing-room supervisor. Gaffney marked this milestone in a letter on 28 October, but at that stage he was still in the dark about when the rest of the staff would be arriving: 'I haven't an idea when the others will be coming out—it's impossible to say when the huts will be ready for them. Exactly a week ago we had the first lavatory installed and believe it or not it made some of the boys sort of "homesick"! So did the sight of two bottles of stout which Fitzgerald and Stewart had included in their luggage! With

A hospital of wooden huts

regard to the former cause of homesickness, our Housekeeper in Chief, Madame Pilorget, observed its installation with undisguised approval, described the new "apparatus" to any new visitors who happened to call to see us and I think went so far as to refer to it as "*magnifique*"!' Baths were harder to come by, and a half dozen of them were only secured the following spring, with the help of the French Red Cross; they were transferred from demolished houses in Paris.

Transport problems continued to try the patience of the Irish staff. Jim Gaffney's letters frequently mention breakdowns, and spare parts had to be ordered from Dublin. After an American party one night, twelve miles from Saint-Lô, the Ford van refused to start, and three of the hospital staff set off on foot. Samuel Beckett walked all the way home, while his two companions gave up and slept by the roadside. On another evening, Beckett and Tommy Dunne walked from Bayeux, a distance of twenty miles, after missing a French Red Cross driver who was to bring them home. Some months later, the United Nations unit at Granville provided the hospital with a sturdy truck on long-term loan. This useful vehicle, which never broke down, could take twelve to fourteen persons on board, was open at the back and had double doors fitted by the hospital's carpenter.

Another problem was the abundance and daring of the rats that had plagued the town since the bombing. Dr Leahy recalls doing night-time security duty at the hospital stores on the stud-farm, with rats running around. The late Nurse Angela Buckley remembered finding two rats eating the butter one morning, in a ward. All sorts of attempts were made to get rid of the problem, which was especially serious in the maternity and children's wards.

As well as patients, their relatives and friends, a constant stream of visitors showed up at the hospital, especially in the early months. The Irish hospital's reputation for hospitality quickly established itself. The matron's recollection that 'no

Healing amid the ruins

stranger I think, ever passed without calling and all received the hospitality of the house' is echoed by one local inhabitant, Raymond Lelièvre, who reported: 'The Hospital doesn't just welcome patients, it is also glad to receive visits from inquisitive folk like myself. My first acquaintance with the wonderful people of Ireland came about while drinking each other's health with glasses of whiskey, the Irish equivalent of calvados.' The task of taking visitors on a tour of the place was designated as a full-time job in itself, as Gaffney noted: 'we have decided that we shall have a "house officer" whose main duty will be to stay all day on the premises and look after those visitors who call to see us. It's a pleasant enough job taking them round and showing them our equipment (which is first-class and far before anything they have here) but it's time-consuming and so we will share the job.'

Many of those who called were journalists and broadcasters, from France and Ireland or from further afield. A couple of delegations came from Scotland, as the city of Perth had adopted Saint-Lô after the war. After being shown around the town and embryonic hospital in October 1945, Miss E. M. Stirling, the Secretary of the Perth French Association, reported that what Saint-Lô most needed was 'clothes, shoes, blankets, furniture, equipment for schools, sports and canteens, tools for the workmen, and black cloth and Latin testaments for the clergy'. Clearly, medical supplies were well covered by this stage.

The first group of nurses arrived at the end of November. As well as the nurse-radiographer, Julia Murphy, this party included nurses Mary Fitzpatrick, Margaret Martin, Eileen Mullally and Anne M. O'Reilly, maternity sister Ita Maeve MacDermott, and sisters Margaret Doherty and Nora Cunningham. Also travelling with them were Dr Tim Boland, the obstetrician and gynaecologist, and Dorothy Smith, who was to act as the hospital's administrator, while the post of assistant matron had been taken up the previous week by Kathleen Conroy.

A hospital of wooden huts

By early December the outpatients department had received over a thousand cases, and the wards opened for inpatients later the same month. By that stage the hospital had six doctors, ten nurses and nine administrative and technical staff.

In the days leading up to Christmas, news arrived that Colonel McKinney's wife was dangerously ill; he returned to Dublin, but his wife had died of a stroke before he arrived home. An obituary mass for her was celebrated in the local parish in Saint-Lô, and this was attended by the mayor and two deputy mayors, as well as the president of the local French Red Cross. Jim Gaffney stood in as acting director of the hospital. He found the administrative work very time-consuming: 'Deputising for the Director has the great disadvantage (from my professional point of view) that I don't have much time to spend in the lab. doing the work I know most about.' McKinney's return early in the new year was a relief.

The hospital's matron, Mary Crowley, arrived in the snow on Christmas Eve 1945, after a rough crossing and a long delay. She was met at Dieppe by Beckett, who drove her '200 miles through snow, via Bailey bridges, landmines and wartime conditions' to arrive in Saint-Lô just in time to hear midnight mass in the bombed-out church of Notre Dame, with violins playing and snow falling through its gaping roof.

A second batch of young nurses, eight strong, sailed for France on 5 January 1946. Other arrivals in early January included Dr Edward Gumbrielle, an anaesthetist, who had graduated from UCD in 1940 and had worked at Dublin's Mater Hospital before training in anaesthetics in Staffordshire; Dr Paddy McNicholas, an ophthalmologist from Galway who had worked in Birmingham, London and Maidstone; and Mr Timmy O'Driscoll, a chemist originally from County Cork.

An American base close by provided the hospital with the services of a chaplain until the arrival of the Irish chaplain, Father Brendan Hynds, in January 1946. Maynooth-trained, Hynds was ordained in 1933 and studied theology for a year at

Healing amid the ruins

the Irish College in Paris. On his ordination, he had spent four years working in the parish of the north Paris suburb of Gennevilliers. (This was in response to an appeal for volunteer clergy from the Archbishop of Paris, who visited Ireland during the Eucharistic Congress of 1932: the Parisian diocese was critically short of priests.)

But Irish staff were not the only newcomers welcomed at the hospital in the new year: in January 1946 the first baby was born in the hospital's maternity ward, and was given the name Patrick Noël.

By 25 January, Jim Gaffney could report a complement of patients which was about half the targeted capacity: 'We are beginning to look really like a hospital now, with somewhere between 45–55 patients.' A sense that order and cleanliness had conquered the mud and chaos emerges from a report by a local French journalist, Albert Desile. He describes being given afternoon tea at the hospital, and being shown around twenty-five spotless snow-white huts, insulated with a brand-new substance called 'isorel', and comfortably laid out, with corridors joining the different departments and fresh flowers adorning the wards and staff dining-room.

Beckett was now coming to the end of his involvement with the Irish hospital. In December 1945, he admits in a letter to Thomas MacGreevy that he finds his work at the hospital exhausting and will be glad to leave: 'And if your experience was anything like mine, you'd be too tired and exasperated at the end of a day of four people talking to you at once, or wanting you at once, to do anything but fall into bed. . . . I anyway am very glad to be going.' He was returning to Paris and considered a request to represent the Irish Red Cross in the capital, but opted in the end to devote himself fully to his writing. 'I thought I would accept, and in fact did unofficially, but feel now like backing out. If I don't feel myself quite free again soon, freedom will never again be any good to me. And with the likelihood of the franc falling I should be able to exist with

A hospital of wooden huts

my pittance, and without the "nominal" salary that I would be getting as their bottlewasher in Paris.' His last task for the hospital, as retiring storekeeper, was to procure rat poison in Paris and to bring it to Saint-Lô in January 1946.

Tommy Dunne, Beckett's assistant, now became storekeeper, but a replacement as interpreter could not be found by the Irish Red Cross. Beckett was also missed as a companion. As Gaffney wrote soon after they started working together: 'He [Beckett] is a most valuable asset to the unit—terribly conscientious about his work and enthusiastic about the future of the hospital, likes a game of bridge and in every way a most likeable chap.' On a visit to Paris 'Sam took me into Notre-Dame which was magnificent. Sam has an assistant storekeeper here named Tommy Dunne, a very decent little Dublin chap. Sam is a TCD graduate, interested in writing and in letters generally; has lived in Paris the last six years or seven; aged about 38-40, no religious persuasion; I should say a free-thinker—but he pounced on a little rosary beads which was on a stall in Notre-Dame to bring back as a little present to Tommy D. It was very thoughtful of him.'

The spring months saw dramatically increasing numbers of both patients and staff. By 6 March the hospital was looking after close on seventy inpatients; a fortnight later, there were over eighty inpatients and over one hundred and twenty outpatients per day; more nurses were expected shortly. On 28 March the number of inpatients exceeded ninety. At the end of March Patrick Carey, a UCD graduate of London-Irish extraction, joined the hospital as first assistant surgeon, from the Royal Infirmary, Leicester.

The fifty-strong staff were kept very busy from this stage on. A second laboratory technician, Roderick Murphy, was recruited for the pathology laboratory, and with queues for the outpatients department starting to form as early as 6.30 am., there was need for more staff in this area too. This need was met by the arrival, in late spring, of an assistant for Dr Darley.

Healing amid the ruins

Dr Kitty Sullivan was the last doctor to join the team. Qualifying in UCD in 1943, she had worked as an intern in St Vincent's Hospital, Dublin, and and had taken a public health course. She had been selected to go to Saint-Lô as early as November 1944, and had been on standby until required. She and Darley were very stretched in the outpatients department, both working long hours without a break and under a good deal of stress.

4: No ramshackle affair

> 'the best that priority can comand'
> *Samuel Beckett*

The Irish hospital was officially inaugurated with much pomp and ceremony—including five official speeches—on 7 April 1946. It was now working almost to its peak capacity and could boast of being one of the best equipped hospitals of its size in France. The inauguration had been planned as far back as December of the previous year. Local public figures, representatives of both the French and Irish governments, and contingents from the Irish Red Cross and the *Croix-Rouge française* were all invited. Scores of guests and local people paraded through the dust and rubble of Saint-Lô's ruined streets, decked with flowers and Irish and French tricolours. The band of the French Fleet from Cherbourg provided music; a banquet hosted by the mayor of the town was followed by a procession to the war memorial, where the national anthems of Ireland and France were played and speeches were made. A tour of inspection of the hospital preceded afternoon tea, a concert and a large ball in the evening.

This was clearly a very moving occasion, and also an exhausting one. For some of those involved, the inauguration was a marathon stretching to close on eighteen hours of celebration. One of Gaffney's letters gives a detailed description of the day:

'The Mass at 9.30 in the nearby Church was well attended by the officers of the municipality and the public. Special places were reserved for the delegates from Dublin and the hospital staff. At the request of the local Curé it was said by Fr Hynds. Afterwards some folks went down having a quick look at the ruins and the rest of us got ready and set off for the banquet,

Healing amid the ruins

timed for about twelve thirty. It was nearly one thirty when we sat down and about three when we stood up. There were about 140 places, nearly all filled, and a good lunch it was. Towards the end we could hear the band playing outside and when we came out the *gendarmerie* were drawn up and the sailors ready with their instruments. We set off in parade down the town to the fast time of a martial air, the sides of the streets lined by an enthusiastic population. At the War Memorial the cortège drew up (that was the French word used), the *gendarmerie* with their rifles on one side, the band of the Fleet on the other. Solemnly a wreath was placed on the grave of the Unknown Soldier and then the band sounded the Last Post.

'This was followed by a very fine, if subdued, rendering of the Soldiers' Song, and then a beautiful playing of the *Marseillaise*. We had, on the request of the Mayor, given a number of large green, white and orange flags for the occasion, and they were plentifully scattered along the route and at the War Memorial. We then took our seats right there and five speeches followed—the Mayor, the Chairman (Mr Maguire), the President of the French Red Cross (General Sicé), the Irish Minister, Mr Murphy, and finally, the Under-Secretary of State for Population.

'More music, and a parade up to the hospital where we drew up just inside the gate. The band and *gendarmerie* drew up as before and the hospital was inaugurated by the green, white and orange being gracefully hoisted by a *gendarme* specially selected for the job, the Soldiers' Song being played the while, and then the French Anthem. Followed an inspection of the hospital by about two hundred people, while the French band were given refreshments in our recreation hut, before going down town again to their open-air concert at 5 p.m. The inspecting party were then given refreshments in the hospital dining-room. That night the band came back and sang songs for us; some went down the town to the Ball which was open to the public and was just packed solid (cement floor and all) and then they came back here and finished with a smaller dance here in our recreation hut, about 3 a.m.'

Some of the French naval band, unaccustomed to the liquid refreshments sent in caseloads by Jameson and Guinness, drank the Irish whiskey neat 'and by the end of the evening they were all laid out on top of or under the tables,' recalled Dr Paddy McNicholas.

During the hospital's heyday in the summer of 1946, one hundred and fifteen beds were filled. The full staff complement comprised a medical director, nine doctors (three medical, two surgical, one anaesthetist, one ophthalmologist, one gynaecologist, and one pathologist), a matron and thirty registered nurses, a chaplain, a chemist, two laboratory technicians, two storekeepers and an administrative staff of nine. Its ambulance service covered most of Normandy.

In June 1946 an Irish Red Cross visitor reported: 'Here was no ramshackle affair, but a group of spacious, well-constructed buildings, laid-out in pleasing design. It is true that the hospital buildings are of wood, but the lower two or three feet are built stone-work, which gives a solid foundation of lasting quality. The wards are wide, roomy and well-ventilated. The ample separation of the beds gives a larger than usual air space to each patient. Centrally-heated throughout, the pavilions are very comfortable. There are at present eighty beds in occupation and the full complement of 100 beds will be in operation very shortly when the additional nurses already selected here have reached Saint-Lô. There will be one nurse to every four patients, a ratio not usually found on the Continent.

'The hospital proper is divided into general, medical, surgical, gynaecological and obstetric units. To the latter there is an excellent labour ward attached. There is also a room adjacent, where the obstetric specialist may sleep so that he can be immediately available when required. There is, in addition, a tuberculosis block, which is not yet fully opened up. The operating theatre is well-lighted naturally, and also by a powerful "Luminaire" day-light lamp. There is a modern oil pump operating table giving all the usual positions. The sterilising and anaesthetic rooms lead off from the theatre. The whole theatre is lined with aluminium sheeting which has a clean, hygienic appearance, in place of the tiling usual here. The effect of working in a metal-lined theatre in hot weather is, however, a matter for further experience. The x-ray room is at present fitted with a portable apparatus which is amply adequate for chest and bone work. The dark room for developing the films is entered directly from the main x-ray room. The laboratory is fully equipped for the purposes of the hospital and will bear favourable comparison, as indeed, will the hospital as a whole, with most of the Dublin voluntary hospitals. It is scarcely necessary, in this connection, to remark that the standards of the Dublin hospitals are among the highest.'

A similar impression of cleanliness and comfort is contained in a piece entitled 'The Capital of the Ruins' that Samuel Beckett wrote for Radio Éireann. The typescript, slightly over three pages in length, bears his signature and is dated 10 June 1946 but there is no record that the piece was ever broadcast.

'On what a year ago was a grass slope, lying in the angle that the Vire and Bayeux roads make as they unite at the entrance of the town, opposite what remains of the second most important stud-farm in France, a general hospital now stands. It is the Hospital of the Irish Red Cross in Saint-Lô, or, as the Laudiniens themselves say, the Irish Hospital. The buildings consist of some 25 prefabricated wooden huts. They are superior, generally speaking, to those so scantily available for the wealthier, the better-connected, the astuter or the more flagrantly deserving of the bombed-out. Their finish, as well without as within, is the best that priority can command. They are lined with glass-wool and panelled in isorel, a strange substance of which only very limited supplies are available. There is real glass in the windows. The consequent atmosphere is that of

No ramshackle affair

brightness and airiness so comforting to sick people, and to weary staffs. The floors, where the exigencies of hygiene are greatest, are covered with linoleum. There was not enough linoleum in France to do more than this. The walls and ceiling of the operating theatre are sheeted in aluminium of aeronautic origin, a decorative and practical solution of an old problem and a pleasant variation on the sword and ploughshare metamorphosis. A system of covered ways connects the kitchen with refectories and wards. The supply of electric current, for purposes both of heat and of power, leaves nothing to be desired.' Later in the piece, Beckett went on to predict that: 'before the town begins to resemble the pleasant and prosperous administrative and agricultural centre that it was, the hospital of wooden huts in its gardens between the Vire and Bayeux roads will continue to discharge its function, and its cured. . . . It will continue to discharge its function long after the Irish are gone and their names forgotten. But I think that to the end of its hospital days it will be called the Irish Hospital . . .'

French observers were warmly complimentary, referring to Ireland's gift of 'this domain of white huts with its bright rooms full of flowers' (*'cette cité blanche, aux salles claires et fleuries'*). The journalist Albert Desile, writing in the *Manche Libre* newspaper thirty years later, still remembered the remarkable equipment that the hospital brought with it, and its meticulous cleanliness. Many tributes were also paid to the architect, M. Lafont.

The cleanliness was at least partly thanks to a dozen or so German prisoners of war from the local POW camp who were assigned to kitchen and general cleaning duties in the hospital. One of them, 'a good German chemist', worked with Gaffney in his laboratory. It was no doubt thanks to these prisoners' constant vigilance that the hospital's shining corridors left a deep impression on the young Maurice Lerebourg, a child-patient, who remembers how easy it was to slip, so highly polished were the linoleum floors.

The town itself was still in ruins. An article in the *Sunday*

Express in July 1946 reported that 'the little emergency railway is still carting away the rubble, in fact the ruins have barely been scraped clean yet. All the same, more than half the pre-bombardment population has already returned, living three to four families together in shaky remnants of houses, in barracks, and in cellars like caves. These Normans have a stubborn affection for their own little plot which no disaster could shake.'

Among those who had returned and were helping to bring life and normality back were Monsieur and Madame Théot who ran the *Café des Ruines*, a favourite haunting place of the Irish. In February 1945 the Théots had come back to Saint-Lô to find their home in the centre of the town destroyed. 'We moved into a ruin at the back of the house . . . It had neither roof nor windows. Snow had fallen all through the month of December. When it melted, it soaked through the walls right down to the floor. The plaster had disappeared and the electric wires hung loose on the walls. Once the roof had been replaced and the windows sealed with "Vitrex" (plastic-coated wire netting used instead of window panes), we moved in to re-open our business: a café-restaurant. Saint-Lô had to get back to normal.

'It was in this café among the ruins that my husband met the Irish. A patient, looking for the hospital, hobbling painfully on his crutches from the station across the ruins, reached our café, which was where the rue Docteur Leturc is today. Seeing him in such distress, my husband took him to the hospital in our car. That was how he met the Irish doctors, because he could speak English and could interpret for the patient he had brought.'

This was the start of a lasting friendship: 'The Irish were happy to find someone they could speak to and became great friends with my husband. We never needed their professional help ourselves, but we often took our friends to them. When they came to us on their days off, they came as friends, not

No ramshackle affair

customers. We often invited them to lunch: they loved French cooking and it was the least we could do.'

Until the town was reconstructed, which took the best part of two decades, the people were housed in prefabricated wooden huts, laid out in provisional wooden housing estates. The first of these estates was erected by August 1946. As in other bombed European towns, such huts became the standard accommodation of those whose homes had been destroyed in the war. The work of acquiring, clearing and preparing sites, and then setting up the huts, was time-consuming and labour intensive. At one stage, three thousand workers and two thousand prisoners of war were involved in this reconstruction process in Saint-Lô.

Kees Van Hoek, the *Sunday Express* journalist, recorded his impressions in July 1946: 'Amid all this endless expanse of gaping ruins, these mountains of rubble, these summer dusts of powdered masonry, the Irish Hospital appears like the fata morgana of a palmy oasis in a barren, scorched desert. Yet it is nothing but a dozen one-storey wooden barracks on stone foundations. But the new white paint looks so clean and the neatly trimmed grounds so freshly green and full of flowers, that in all its utilitarian simplicity Normandy's "Irishtown" appears positively luxurious.'

Most of the hospital's patients came from Saint-Lô and its neighbouring areas; some came from as far away as Rouen, Dieppe and Paris. Apart from the normal cases that would be expected in a town the size of Saint-Lô, many came who were suffering from scabies and other skin conditions due to the effects of malnutrition and an ill-balanced wartime diet. Roundworms were also a chronic problem.

The surgical unit had very up-to-date equipment and twenty-six special surgical beds. It was kept very busy. There were recurring casualties from crumbling buildings and exploding mines. From the surrounding countryside, farmers were often admitted with limbs blown off. 'Accident cases are frequent. Masonry falls when least expected, children play with detonators and demining continues', as Beckett reported in June 1946. One of these child casualties was an eleven-year-old boy who had to lose at least three fingers of his right hand because of contact with a small grenade while playing in a meadow. But children will meet with accidents even where there are no explosive devices lying around. Paddy Carey recalled an emergency tracheostomy which he successfully performed on a child who had drunk boiling liquid. The eight-year-old Maurice Lerebourg must have been one of the unit's longest staying patients. As a result of knocking a vessel of boiling water over himself, he spent six months in the Irish hospital from July to December 1946. Suffering from severe third degree burns, he was treated with morphine and penicillin and was in a coma for three weeks before undergoing skin grafts along his left arm and abdomen. Over fifty years later, M. Lerebourg still remembers the Irish staff who saved his life, and the shining, slippery floors.

When the young Daniel Couvez was admitted with meningitis, Desmond Leahy successfully performed a tricky lumbar puncture and treated the boy with penicillin. His mother was so grateful to the Irish doctor for saving her son's life that when her next child, a daughter, was born she called the baby 'Desmonde' after Leahy, who was also asked to be the child's godfather.

The paediatric section had ten cots and two side wards and, with its bright colourful decoration, resembled a nursery more than a hospital. The children responded so well to treatment that there was usually a quick turnover of patients.

The tuberculosis wards comprised two huts of ten cubicles each. All its patients were men, many of whom had been interned or in concentration camps during the war. This department was ready early in 1946, but the matron refused to open it because there were not enough nursing staff to cover it. So the doctors volunteered to do night duty in shifts: Desmond

No ramshackle affair

Leahy remembers walking up and down the TB wards at night, until extra nurses came out from Ireland. When the ward was opened, Dr Jean Bourdon, the local tuberculosis specialist, treated patients in it.

Patients expressed their gratitude in kind with gifts of food, bottles of calvados and invitations to family meals. 'On market day,' wrote Gaffney, 'a lady came with her son to Darley's Out-Patient Department. Said she had a chicken for him in her basket. She had some shopping to do; would leave the basket there and call for it later. An hour later Arthur was surprised to find a live chicken jumping around the pharmacy. He assumed she had brought it dead. There's never any shortage of flowers, beautiful roses, rhododendrons, lilies, sweet pea, etc.' Madame Rosalie Lecluse once offered the hospital the present of a goose. Regular choice cuts came from the Delannoës' butchers' shop, after Madame Cécile Delannoë had spent a month in the hospital, in the autumn of 1946. Dr Boland had operated on her and she was very grateful to him for sitting up through the night with her. Many other former patients speak with great warmth of Dr Boland, who was a man of considerable charm.

Communication between locals and Irish staff with imperfect school French did not seem to pose any insuperable problems. Some of the Red Cross nurses had attended intensive French classes before going to Saint-Lô, as had some doctors. Angela Buckley remembered that she used a few standard phrases and managed to get through to the patients all right. The patients, for their part, were constantly being asked to speak slowly to the Irish staff. Former patients admit that there was some mutual incomprehension, but that this did not matter. One woman, who often invited the Irish around to her home, remembers that they could not understand a word of each other's remarks, but she has a fond memory of a Christmas gathering where everybody ended up singing the one song they all knew in Latin, the *Adeste Fideles*.

Healing amid the ruins

Right from the beginning of their stay in France, Colonel McKinney encouraged his staff to take part in local activities. He saw social relations as essential to the success of the project and insisted that the staff's expenses should be reimbursed. As a result, the Irish attended race meetings, concerts and dances, some held in support of local men returning home from captivity or forced labour in Germany. There was an element of official representation in these outings which may sometimes have been constraining: Angela Buckley remembered being invited to go beagling, or to victory dances, and resenting having to wear her uniform. Jim Gaffney attended, in an official capacity, the 14th of July parade and wreath-laying ceremony at the town's war memorial.

The Red Cross organisation offered opportunities for social contacts, at local level and further afield. When they went up to Paris, the Irish doctors often met representatives from the *Croix-Rouge française*, and business gatherings with their French counterparts would be extended to outings to the theatre or the opera, to concerts and visits to the Louvre. On one visit in September, Gaffney and Beckett were dinner guests in the family home of the hospital architect, Monsieur Lafont.

Nearer to Saint-Lô, the Manche branch of the French Red Cross showed enormous hospitality to the Irish visitors. The regional President, the Comte de Kergorlay of the castle of Canisy, had put up the first Irish contingent for a few days. Later, in the spring of 1946, the Kergorlay seaside villa at Coutainville was made available to the Irish hospital staff for holidays. About twenty-five miles away, the villa was a boon to the Irish nurses and doctors during the heat of the summer months. Standing in its own grounds, with twelve bedrooms accommodating seventeen people, it became a regular destination for weekends off duty. 'The beach is like Rosses Point . . . ' wrote Gaffney, 'I heard them say the water is lukewarm all the time.' The cooking was excellent according to Dr Desmond Leahy, thanks to Madame Pilorget, the former Red Cross nurse

No ramshackle affair

and housekeeper at the Irish hospital who transferred to Coutainville. She had frequent difficulties containing the mirth of the Irish *jeunesse débordante de vitalité* (youth overflowing with zest for life).

As well as several US Army camps, the area contained an American Relief to Europe base at Coutances, a UN unit at Granville, and RAF and RAMC units in Bayeux. There was much co-operation between these different agencies, and relations between them and the Irish were excellent. Gaffney describes a visit to a local US camp where he and his companions greatly appreciated a hot shower before a visit to a nearby convent: 'We got over there on Tuesday, the padre took us to his Nissen hut, electric lighting and central heating etc., gave us a drink and then six of us had a fine shower with very hot water followed by a cold drenching. Back to his hut and then with a few friends of his, divided ourselves between our ambulance and a jeep. Off about ten miles to a magnificent château where the Rev. Mother welcomed us and gave a seven-course dinner to the whole eleven of us; got around the piano afterwards and sang for further orders till about one a.m. They want us to come again to have a real look around and we promised to do so (the nuns that is). Dr Thompson and Beckett [who were both Protestant] said they hadn't thought that convents were such nice places.'

A visit to the American hospital near Cherbourg impressed Gaffney: 'Tuesday Sam and I were taken by Fr Bardeck to see the 196th General Hospital (US). Imagine 196 hospitals, each with three times the number of beds (and therefore equipment) that the Mater has. They still look after their 1,500 beds but are closing down fairly soon. It is up near Cherbourg about 55 miles from here, and is only about 13 miles from one of the D-day landing beaches—Omaha beach. . . . We enjoyed our visit, were given dinner and an invitation to come and stay the night any time.'

They bumped into Irish-Americans in Paris, too, as Gaffney

reports in early October, 1945: 'Paris is still full of US personnel—own the best hotels, rent the best cinemas and theatres and own most of the traffic on the streets; it's most impressive. Dawdling outside the [Madeleine] church we were approached by a soldier who told us he was back from Donegal where his "people" came from. Another came up—Mr. O'Neill from Boston, Mass.—who is trying "like hell" to get to Ireland.'

Hospitality also came from the British in Paris: 'Recently the medical staff here were made honorary members of the British Officers Club in Paris which is said to be the best in Europe. . . . it was built for Madame Pompadour; and since the invasion has been given indefinitely to HM Government by the owner, one of the Rothschilds. We are very pleased to be members, if only for the fact that a good dinner costs the equivalent of 3s as it's run on non-profit lines. . . . The Club is beside the British Embassy.'

The staff became very friendly with an RAF unit nearby: 'An RAF unit, very small, moved into Bayeux recently, twenty miles away. Two of them looked in one day, Squadron Leader Foster, British, who has seen a few rugger matches in Dublin, and Fl/Lt. Lord from Montreal. They are part of the War Graves Commission—trying to trace the graves of 30,000 airmen, parachutists, etc. lost over this part of France. Among them (about twelve in all) are New Zealanders and Australians. One of the latter dropped in the other day. "What", he said: "a cup of real Irish tea in a real Irish hospital in France! Wait till I tell my folks about this—you know, my parents come from County Clare".'

The Irish hospital itself hosted many parties in its recreation hut. A table tennis table from an American camp was installed there, and this was a popular pastime, with the hospital staff once fielding their own team to play against a local team in the town. The hut was also used for dances, which became a regular feature of life at the hospital, with Maurice Fitzgerald presiding as the bilingual master of ceremonies.

No ramshackle affair

Former patients remember the dances as 'wild'. Men were invited from the British and American camps nearby. A large dance was held there just after Christmas 1945, for staff and their friends. It was a great success, partly because, as Gaffney remarks, their younger French friends were 'easy to entertain— as would anyone be indeed, who hadn't been to a dance for six–seven years; or been allowed to. Some of the nurses and ourselves sang some Irish songs which interested our visitors very much.' The St Patrick's Day, 17 March 1946, dance was a large affair, attended by about eighty people and lasting until the early hours of the following morning. American, British and French visitors were invited, and music was provided by radio and gramophone pickup.

Indeed, the Irish reputation for knowing how to enjoy themselves seems to have been well demonstrated by some reports. Hints of wild behaviour on their time off can be gleaned from some entries in nurses' autograph albums, as is to be expected in a large group of unattached young people, tasting something of the irresponsibility of being abroad for the first time in their lives. A non-drinker herself, Angela Buckley recalled with amazement how much cider, wine and calvados could be consumed by her countrymen during their time off; Samuel Beckett remembered quite a lot of drinking going on, and evenings whiled away in a local brothel. He advised MacGreevy against coming to Saint-Lô, as he felt that his friend would not appreciate the atmosphere of 'promiscuity' and 'intemperance among the ruins'.

The Irish visitors were invited to weddings and attended funerals. Former patients remember Arthur Darley's violin-playing in many homes, where he was at times accompanied on the piano by *le grand Sam*, Samuel Beckett. The *joie de vivre* of the staff was infectious; the nurses were always singing.

The staff at the nearby stud-farm, where the hospital supplies were stored, also became very friendly with the Irish, and there was much coming and going in both directions. A Christmas party for children was planned by Dr Gaffney, while he was acting director, but this idea was dropped as Colonel McKinney was not in favour of it. Instead, the Irish distributed sweets and toys to children attending local children's parties at the *gendarmerie*: 'the Chief of Police has invited us (the five medical personnel) to the police HQ on the afternoon of Christmas Day to a children's party where 270 of the children of the police are to be entertained. He is a most pleasant chap and thinks we are a godsend to the town. We have also been asked to look in at another children's "do"—the *arbre de Noël*. Yes, 'Christmas tree'—on Sunday next for children over three; and another on Christmas Eve afternoon for those under three.' Children from the neighbourhood came to play in the hospital grounds, and afternoon tea on Sundays became a regular feature. The mayor, Georges Lavalley, the *préfet* and the *sous-préfet* were very friendly towards the hospital.

In sum, the hospital had become a local institution in postwar Saint-Lô. The town, with its postwar population of five or six thousand people, was one to which many of the Irish team, coming themselves from small towns or rural backgrounds, could readily relate. It was all the more upsetting, therefore, when the underlying tensions between the local doctors, the Red Cross in Paris and the Irish hospital erupted in what came to be known as *l'affaire de l'hôpital irlandais*. A bitter public controversy resulted in two doctors resigning their seats on the town council, other councillors threatening to resign, and a massive street demonstration in support of the Irish medical staff. We shall see in the next chapter what lay behind these events.

5: The *affaire de l'hôpital irlandais*

> 'Whose exceptionally pia
> Mater hatched this grand idea
> Is not known.'
> *Samuel Beckett*

The *hôpital irlandais* had been established to meet the medical needs of a war-devastated town, painfully reconstructing itself. It was never intended that the hospital should have any permanent Irish involvement—this would have been neither desirable nor feasible. However, the circumstances of the Irish departure from the town were most unfortunate and left a lasting impression among many of the citizens of Saint-Lô that the Irish had been forced to leave prematurely by the ingratitude and selfish machinations of local French doctors. Contemporary local editions of *Ouest-France* and *Manche Libre* report that the Irish staff were forced to pull out of Saint-Lô much earlier than intended, and against the entreaties of the mayor, the municipal council, and the people of the town.

There is a good deal of truth in this version of events, but the matter was more complicated than the reports imply. Things were happening behind the scenes unbeknownst to those most caught up in the drama.

In the first place, the Irish Red Cross was running out of money to finance the hospital. From the outset, successive fundraising appeals had stated that the length of time the hospital would be maintained by the Irish Red Cross would depend on the generosity of the Irish people. In the second place, the duration of its involvement in Saint-Lô, and the date at which it was to hand over to the French, had never been settled and this was a source of understandable concern to the local French doctors. They needed to re-establish their practices on a pre-war footing but this was impossible for them, as long as the *hôpital irlandais* continued to operate under Irish Red Cross management, providing free treatment, and failing, as they saw it, to operate within the agreed guidelines. Such clashes are regular features of aid projects which often upset the local balance of economic and social interests. As a member of *Médecins sans Frontières* notes: 'The presence of the "foreign" team upsets the normal hierarchy and power relations in the hospital. Doctors are hit hardest as the "foreign" teams provide care free of charge, thus affecting their incomes, while nurses often appreciate the additional training, attention and salaries. Although local politicians or medical authorities are often pleased to take credit for the intervention, the local doctors are rarely as excited.' The Saint-Lô doctors attempted to force the issue, but in such an inept and indeed duplicitous way, that as events unfolded they were caused the maximum amount of embarrassment at local level.

'About two years' had been the period understood by Alan Thompson for the involvement of the Irish Red Cross in Saint-Lô but the starting-point for calculating those two years is not clear. Jim Gaffney writes in the middle of July 1946 that 'it looks as if the Irish will stay here till about next March or April, hardly longer' yet just over a fortnight later he reports a much earlier date of departure for the Irish staff, mentioning 'a letter from Head Office saying that the Society will be handing the hospital over to the French Red Cross on October 31st, next.'

Complicating the matter was a proposal, during the early summer of 1946, to establish a similar Irish Red Cross hospital in Warsaw. The matron, Mary Crowley, recalled how the 'feat of transhipping a hundred-bed hospital complete' had impressed numerous foreign visitors to the *hôpital irlandais*, and that requests had often been made for 'the establishment of similar

The *affaire de l'hôpital irlandais*

hospitals in other war torn areas'. One such request had come from the Polish Red Cross, and the Irish branch explored the possibility with some enthusiasm. Colonel McKinney, who had been refused leave to stay in Saint-Lô beyond 3 May, and had been replaced by Dr Leahy, was granted leave to travel to Warsaw in June 1946 to examine the feasibility of setting up another hospital there.

He was accompanied, as on the previous year's journey to Paris and northern France, by the architect Michael Scott. Scott recalled an arduous journey through Zurich and Prague before arriving in Warsaw to find it over ninety per cent destroyed. He and the Colonel spent much of their time in the ruined capital waiting around with no apparent business to transact, but finally (through chance) succeeded in having a meeting with the Polish Ministers for Agriculture and Health. The *Irish Press* carried a report from Warsaw on 22 June, in which Colonel McKinney was allegedly planning a hospital on the same scale as the one in Normandy, with one hundred beds and a large outpatients department. Like the French hospital, the Polish one was to be entirely equipped and mainly staffed from Ireland. It was hoped that it would be opened the following winter.

Meanwhile, in the Saint-Lô hospital, some of the Irish staff, who had heard exaggerated rumours about the state of progress in the Polish project, considered applying to serve in Warsaw. Jim Gaffney writes on 21 June, for instance, that 'many of the staff here are interested in going there, and are just anxious to know when it's coming off. It's said here that the equipment etc. has already been purchased and it only remains for the personnel to be recruited and a site to be found.' But the staff were not kept closely informed. At the end of July he remarks in another letter: 'No official news of Warsaw since and the staff here are still very anxious to know if it's really coming off.' That the Warsaw plan was connected, in Gaffney's mind, to the Irish staff's departure date from Saint-Lô is clear in another letter written in late August: 'There's still little news of the [future of the] Unit or of the next one [in Warsaw] but we are expecting some soon.'

In the end, the Warsaw plan never got off the ground. The *Irish Press* reporter outlined some of the reasons: 'Provision of a site and a suitable building, which is the only responsibility the Poles will have, will be one of the major problems in view of the devastation of the city, where it seems impossible to move without seeing or stumbling over wreckage. . . . Building materials in Warsaw are, probably, more scarce than in any other part of the world to-day. . . . The problems facing the Irish Red Cross personnel, who will man this hospital, promise to be five hundred times greater than those at Saint-Lô . . . The problem of getting supplies to this second hospital of the Irish Society will be a complex one, as they will have to travel across Europe instead of across a narrow channel as is the case at Saint-Lô.'

Michael Scott viewed the Warsaw mission as a completely futile exercise. He described the Irish Red Cross committee as 'well-meaning and dedicated people, but they don't seem to be well organised' and summarised the difficulties involved in setting up an Irish hospital in an eastern block régime. 'The hospital never went ahead. We couldn't finance it first of all, we had no currency relationship with the communist world. We had no means of protecting our people; we didn't recognise the Polish government. Anyway, the Russians had taken over and we didn't recognise them either, so it was impossible.'

Other, ideological, difficulties were hinted at in an extract from an External Affairs minute of 28 January 1947, signed by Michael MacWhite, which reports a visit to Iveagh House by the Assistant General of the African Missions, a Father Collins, who 'in the course of the conversation referred to the transfer of the staff of Saint-Lô Hospital to Warsaw. He thought that by this move the Irish Red Cross was playing into the hands of Bolshevik propagandists. The . . . fact that they are

The *affaire de l'hôpital irlandais*

from Catholic Ireland will be used as a proof in Europe and America that the Polish authorities are not hostile to the Catholic Church.' Such a glimpse into the thinking of the early cold war period suggests that, even if the Warsaw project had been financially viable, it would not have been easy for the Irish Red Cross successfully to carry it out. In any case, an Irish Red Cross envoy reported after travelling to Czechoslovakia and Poland in January 1947 his impression that the Poles did not particularly require a hospital, and would 'find a factory much more welcome!'

The Warsaw project was all the more bizarre given the state of the Irish Red Cross's finances. By the spring of 1946 the Saint-Lô hospital had already cost over £40,000. Estimated running costs (excluding salaries) were in the order of £50,000 for six months, and staffing cost from £1,100 to £2,000 per month.

That the public was not being quite generous enough is suggested by continuing appeals for funds. In spring 1946, the society's chairman explained why the Irish Red Cross was unable to set up a hospital in Belgrade, as requested. 'Saint-Lô . . . ' wrote Conor Maguire, 'has cost about £50,000. As its services are free its continuing strain upon our resources will be heavy. In view of other expenditure at home and abroad we cannot calculate on maintaining the Hospital beyond another six months. For Anti-Tuberculosis work we must earmark £50,000. We still have with us 100 French children. We are planning to equip the Home at Glencree. These plans will require more than the balance of the £160,000 provided by the public. . . . So our first difficulty with regard to Belgrade arises from lack of funds.'

The chairman's reference to pressing public health needs on the home front was by no means casual. In the 1940s, Ireland had the most severe tuberculosis problem in Western Europe, with mortality from the disease sharply increasing during the war years, and the Irish Red Cross had been enlisted as a pivotal organisation in the national campaign to combat it. In addition, there was chronic typhoid to be tackled, and high infant and maternal mortality rates.

Even more significantly, the other source of funding, through sweepstakes held for the benefit of the Irish Red Cross, was now closed. The 1939 Public Hospitals (No. 2) Act had authorised the Red Cross sweepstakes only 'during the continuance of the present European War'. An attempt to persuade the Irish Government to introduce legislation allowing the society to retain in peacetime its powers to raise funds through sweepstakes was unsuccessful.

In any event, revenue from the Irish sweeps organisation—which had provided a constant flow of vast sums of money for hospital development during the 1930s—saw a dramatic downturn during the war years, with ticket sales in Britain and other countries plummeting, and major race meetings being called off. Moreover, any profits generated would be needed for the Irish public health reform strategy of 1945.

So the special wartime status of the society, allowing it to be a beneficiary of sweepstakes funding, had drawn to an end at precisely the time when its needs for funding were most acute—the moment when the Saint-Lô project was getting under way.

For financial reasons alone, therefore, the departure of the Irish was likely to be sooner rather than later. However, the manner in which they eventually did leave Saint-Lô brought to the surface certain underlying tensions in the town and, almost despite itself, the hospital became embroiled in a local political scandal, the so-called *affaire de l'hôpital irlandais,* as it was dubbed during the autumn of 1946. The tensions that surfaced, involving essentially three main vested interests with a stake in the future of the hospital, were those between the town of Saint-Lô and the French Red Cross, between local French doctors and the municipal authorities, and between local doctors and the Irish hospital.

Rumours, circulating in the town since early summer 1946,

The *affaire de l'hôpital irlandais*

about the imminent departure of the Irish medical staff, were confirmed on 3 August, when Dr Gaffney and Dr Leahy requested a meeting with Georges Lavalley, the mayor of Saint-Lô. They had received news from Dublin of a decision, taken by the Irish Red Cross executive committee on 26 July, that the society would hand over the hospital to the French Red Cross in three months' time, on 31 October. The decision followed a visit to the hospital by surgeon C. J. MacAuley, who had gone to Saint-Lô in July at the executive committee's request, and submitted an extensive report on all of the hospital's departments.

M. Lavalley informed his colleagues of this decision at a meeting of the municipal council two days later, on 5 August. The council unanimously regretted the Irish Red Cross's decision, which had been made without the prior agreement of the town and which would so suddenly deprive the people of Saint-Lô of the excellent care which they had been receiving at the hospital. In addition, the council members passed a resolution that the Irish Red Cross Society be asked, through the Irish Minister in Paris, to reconsider its decision and to keep the Irish staff on in Saint-Lô for at least one more year, until 31 October 1947.

Approaches were duly made to the Irish Red Cross. The mayor and another member of the council travelled to Paris to meet Mr Murphy, the Irish Minister. The mayor wrote to Mr de Valera, as Irish Minister for External Affairs, on 17 August, pleading, on behalf of the people of Saint-Lô, the postponement of the Irish withdrawal from the hospital. But Dublin's response was essentially the same: the decision to hand over the hospital on 31 October still stood. The society's reply was accompanied by an enclosure which greatly increased M. Lavalley's alarm, and added fuel to the flames of emotion mounting among members of the town council. The enclosure was a copy of a resolution from the *syndicat des Médecins de la Manche*, the local branch of the French medical union, which made it clear that local doctors would prefer the Irish to leave the hospital as soon as possible.

The medical union's resolution had been discussed at two meetings, in Saint-Lô at the end of May and in Coutances on 22 July 1946, and was sent to the Irish Red Cross headquarters in August. With France's return to full sovereignty French doctors were both able and willing to treat their own people again; and so, it was argued, hospitals in France should be run by French administrators and French medical personnel. They therefore requested the immediate transfer of the Irish hospital to French control. While thanking the Irish people for their humanitarian gesture in France's time of need, the Manche doctors also expressed their hope that the justice of their request would be understood by their colleagues across the sea.

Two incidents point to the source of the local doctors' frustration. M. Marcel Menant, who lived beside the Irish hospital, remembered overhearing a couple of farmers going by in their cart one day, talking about the Irish hospital and exclaiming in their local patois how a visit there cost nothing. A similar anecdote is reported by Raymond Lelièvre, concerning a local country woman who, when feeling unwell and told by her own doctor that she was not ill enough to be hospitalised, retorted by declaring that she would call for an Irish hospital ambulance, because the Irish would come and collect her as they did everyone who asked them.

The medical union's resolution infuriated Lavalley and other council members. However, what incensed them even more was the fact that two members of the council, Doctors Jean Bourdon and Albert Philippe, had been involved in drawing up the doctors' demand and had kept quiet about it, when the council was drafting its own resolution on 5 August, pleading for a postponement of the Irish departure.

Georges Lavalley called an extraordinary meeting of the council which met on Tuesday 17 September. Informing councillors of the recent developments—the reply from the Irish

The *affaire de l'hôpital irlandais*

Red Cross confirming their date of departure at the end of October and the resolution adopted by the medical union— the mayor criticised the two doctors Bourdon and Philippe, for not mentioning the resolution at the previous council meeting. In defence of their position, Dr Bourdon explained at length the various reasons behind the medical union's demand, including the fact that the Irish doctors had failed to comply with the guidelines on admission drawn up the previous winter. Insults, accusations and counter-accusations flew. It was even alleged, in a lengthy debate, that the Saint-Lô branch of the doctors' union had refused to treat the sick mother-in-law of a councillor, M. Louis Gablin, because the latter had taken issue with Dr Bourdon over the *hôpital irlandais*. It was also rumoured, by Dr Bourdon, that the French Red Cross had persuaded their Irish counterparts not to sign an agreement drawn up in Paris in November 1945, between officials from the Public Health Ministry, the Irish Red Cross and the French Red Cross, to transfer ownership of the hospital to the town rather than the French Red Cross.

This agreement stipulated a three-month interregnum, during which the French Red Cross would control the hospital, and after which the ownership would be handed over to a local body. Although Colonel McKinney had agreed in principle, ratification of the agreement was apparently being blocked by the French Red Cross. Dr Bourdon suggested that the newly appointed French Red Cross President, General Sicé, was not happy with the terms laid down in November, as he had made remarks to this effect during a recent visit to the town.

After a long and bruising debate, the meeting mandated the mayor to go to Dublin with a petition from the people of the town asking the Irish to remain, and also to ask that the Irish Red Cross ratify the November agreement. In that way, the town of Saint-Lô woud be sure of inheriting the hospital shortly after a future Irish withdrawal.

Following this meeting a demonstration was organised in

Healing amid the ruins

the town to protest against the Irish withdrawal. Local branches of the main unions and commercial organisations as well as other groups placed notices in the newspapers urging the public to take to the streets on Saturday 21 September at 5.30 p.m. Businesses were asked to close half an hour early, to allow as many of their employees as possible to take part in the demonstration to show the population's appreciation of the Irish staff, and to ask that the *hôpital irlandais* continue in its present form.

Nearly five thousand people marched in the protest. They represented a broad range of social groups, including municipal councillors from Saint-Lô and elsewhere in the Manche area, the police, employer organisations and trade unions, and associations which had grown up during and after the war, such as the *Comité de Libération, the Comité de Défense des Sinistrés, Entr'Aide Française*, veteran soldiers and returned prisoners. Banners carried slogans such as *'Vive l'Irlande!', 'Reconnaissance aux Irlandais!', 'Saint-Lô a encore besoin de vous!'* Speeches were made, to tumultuous applause. A resolution was passed unanimously that Doctors Bourdon and Philippe should be asked to resign from the town council. M. Lavalley promised the crowd that he would go to Ireland to plead the cause. He also stressed the need for the crowd to show some dignity, so that the Irish would be able to tell their countrymen that the people of Saint-Lô knew how to say 'thank you'. A long and disciplined procession marched to the Irish hospital where flowers were presented to the staff from all the various groups assembled, and warm expressions of gratitude were heard. The crowd then marched back to the town hall, where the mayor was entrusted with a petition containing over two thousand signatures, to present to the Irish government during his forthcoming visit to Ireland.

Lavalley travelled to Dublin on 23 September and met Colonel McKinney and a representative of the Irish government. On his return, he called another extraordinary meeting

The *affaire de l'hôpital irlandais*

of the town council, to relay the result of his meeting. He had been very touched by the welcome extended to him: '*J'ai été véritablement touché de la sympathie, de l'affection que ces gens-là ont pour nous.*' It had been made clear to him that the Irish Red Cross could not finance a prolonged presence in Saint-Lô; nevertheless he obtained a reprieve of two months, and the departure date for the Irish staff was now set at 31 December 1946. The problem of ownership of the hospital was also cleared up in Dublin with the ratification of the November agreement.

There remained the public relations disaster which the local doctors had created for themselves. Their letter to the Irish Red Cross seeking an immediate Irish withdrawal had been unnecessary: the Irish lacked the money to prolong their stay. The medical union, the *syndicat des Médecins de la Manche*, published a very long press statement a couple of days after the townspeople's demonstration of 21 September. It reaffirmed the union's confidence in its members, Doctors Bourdon and Philippe, and laid out the reasons behind its attitude to the Irish presence in Saint-Lô. These came under four headings: legal, social, financial and technical. In the first place, it was argued that, now that France was on her feet again after the war, foreign doctors wishing to practise in France must by law have a French qualification. The social argument held that the hospital should be confined to the Saint-Lô area, and not admit patients from other departments; beds should be reserved for the less well-off and should not be taken up by people who could afford to be treated in private clinics. The smaller French hospital in the town, the Saint-Joseph hospital, was losing financially, since no health insurance contributions were being collected as long as the Irish Red Cross was supplying a free service; and this meant that there would be a large deficit in the funds available for health expenditure after the Irish departed. Finally, the technical inadequacies of the Irish hospital were listed: it had only twenty medical and ten paediatric beds, and could not properly treat typhoid and diphtheria cases.

Healing amid the ruins

This statement, while it helped to convince the Irish of the justice of the local doctors' 'very reasonable attitude' (as Beckett had described their position a year before), did nothing to endear them to their fellow citizens. At a further meeting of the municipal council, on 2 October, the quarrel between the mayor, Georges Lavalley, and the two doctors, Jean Bourdon and Albert Philippe, came to a head. The level of debate was as acrimonious as on occasions the previous month, and various councillors threatened to resign, including the mayor himself, if the two doctors did not immediately tender their resignation from the council. Placed under this pressure, the two men did resign, but continued to defend their honour in public during the ensuing weeks by communicating their point of view to the press, which also ran replies from Lavalley.

Financial and medical realities dictated the Irish departure from Saint-Lô. However, the ill-tempered debate did at least achieve three worthwhile objectives: the Irish staff provided two extra months' free service to the population, there was a smooth transition during this period, and the principle of local municipal control of the hospital was established.

The hospital staff was largely unaffected by the storm brewing around it in the town, although the nurses, who had closer contacts with the patients than some of the doctors, were more in touch with local news and gossip.

As autumn slipped into winter, and as the debate over the *affaire de l'hôpital irlandais* began to take up less space in the pages of *Manche Libre* and *Ouest-France*, the Irish doctors and nurses began to pack their bags for their homeward journey. During the last two months of 1946, French staff were gradually taken on to fill vacancies as the Irish left, in order to ensure a smooth transition for the hospital management; the French Red Cross was in charge of this local recruitment during this interim period. A French matron was appointed by the middle of November. Many of the existing French staff were re-employed at the hospital, and their posts were negotiated in writ-

The *affaire de l'hôpital irlandais*

ing. By January 1947 the hospital was already under the new local management of the *Commission Administrative de l'Hospice de Saint-Lô*. This body included Doctors Bourdon and Philippe, and was presided over by Lavalley.

A couple of days before the departure for Ireland of the first group of nurses on 5 December, a reception was held in a local school, with many public figures present. A series of moving tributes were paid to the Irish women by Lavalley and others. In his speech the mayor thanked the Irish nurses by referring to their country's magnificent gesture of reaching out a helping hand among the ruins of a small French town. Significantly, Lavalley characterised the Irish action as an act of faith in the future of Saint-Lô itself: *'le geste magnifique de votre pays, ce geste de grande fraternité dans les ruines d'une petite ville de France, est une bien belle page écrite au livre d'or de son histoire et aussi un acte de foi dans l'avenir de Saint-Lô.'* Similarly emotive terms were used on the same occasion by the president of the local *Comité de Défense des Sinistrés*, M. Quévy, who spoke of the bombed-out returning to their ruined town, to find the Irish there to look after them and care for them in their affliction, like attentive companions of the town's resurrection, prompt to treat their wounds—wounds which were psychological as well as physical: *'nous, sinistrés de Saint-Lô, nous ne pouvons pas oublier qu'au début, lorsque nous sommes rentrés dans Saint-Lô en ruines, nous avons trouvé cet Hôpital . . . Vous avez su avec délicatesse, avec affection, vous pencher sur notre douleur. Vous avez été les compagnons attentifs du début de notre résurrection, vous nous avez pansé nos blessures, physiques et morales . . . Et lorsqu'on parlera de la résurrection de Saint-Lô, l'Irlande sera toujours à l'honneur.'* (we, the survivors of Saint-Lô, cannot forget that when we first came back to Saint-Lô in ruins, we found this hospital . . . Delicately, affectionately, you tended our afflictions. You were our caring companions in the first stages of our resurrection, you healed our wounds, both physical and emotional . . . And whenever people talk of the resurrection of

Saint-Lô, Ireland will always deserve special mention . . .')

Lavalley praised their *'œuvre magnifique'* (magnificent work) and their dedication and sensitivity which would never be forgotten by the patients they had cured. In his reply to his French hosts, the ophthalmologist, Dr McNicholas, said that the Irish, not having had to live through the war themselves, considered their work in France to be no more than their duty. The evening ended with everyone standing up and singing *Ma Normandie*, the anthem of the region, which all the Irish staff knew by heart.

A final banquet was held in the Irish hospital itself, on Thursday 19 December 1946. Colonel McKinney was granted a week's leave from 16 to 23 December, to represent the Irish Red Cross Society and to be present at this last formal gathering of the Irish staff at the hospital he had been so instrumental in setting up. The farewell banquet was attended by the entire staff of the hospital, Irish and French, as well as civilian, military and religious representatives. The mayor took advantage of the occasion to confer on Colonel McKinney the title of honorary citizen, *citoyen d'honneur*, of Saint-Lô.

On a foggy morning, the second day of 1947, the bulk of the remaining Irish staff left Saint-Lô, some by train, some in trucks provided by the British Army. A crowd of several hundred people, men, women and children, gathered to see them off at the station. The crowd, composed of official representatives and ordinary wellwishers, 'spontaneously cheered the staff, presented them with flowers, shook hands with them, embraced them and, in many cases, wept.' As the vehicles disappeared out of view, the people of Saint-Lô sadly waved goodbye to the Irish nurses, whose arms were laden with bunches of flowers.

6: As good as they gave

> 'long after the Irish are gone and their names forgotten.'
>
> *Samuel Beckett*

After the Irish staff left, the hospital continued to function under French management until the end of June 1956. The St Paul de Chartres sisters, a French nursing order, took over the day to day running of the hospital. Their own hospital had been destroyed in the bombing. The change of management, however, did not alter the name and, as Samuel Beckett had foretold in June 1946, 'to the end of its hospital days' the hospital of wooden huts was always known as *l'hôpital irlandais*.

It had been envisaged that a permanent hospital building would replace the wooden huts after about five years. But as Beckett had phrased it in his radio broadcast, '"provisional" is not the term it was, in this universe become provisional' and it was to be a decade before the new hospital was ready.

Architects for the new building were approved before the end of 1946 and its foundation stone was laid in July 1948, but the project stalled for various economic reasons, notably the spiralling inflation of the postwar period. An article in *Manche Libre* in early 1952 claimed that funds for building the new hospital had run out, and that the town was in danger of soon having no hospital at all. Meanwhile, the *hôpital irlandais*, which was showing its age, would be past repair within two years. The huts which had been hastily put up in 1945, with an expected lifetime of three to five years, were now unsafe. Partly without proper foundations, some of their timbers were already rotting and they were vulnerable to high winds. Worse, the huts were a fire hazard, given the inflammable material used to build them, and the nature of the electrical installations. The mayor, Georges Lavalley, admitted that he was often haunted by the idea of the hospital catching fire.

Eventually, the delays were overcome, and the brand new hospital, the *Centre Hospitalier Mémorial France États-Unis*, was opened on 10 May 1956. Largely funded by American aid to France, and designed by the American architect, Paul Nelson, this building could not have presented a greater contrast to the Irish hospital, in terms not only of size, but also of architectural innovation, material equipment and state-of-the-art technology. The new hospital was dedicated to the memory of the American soldiers and others who had lost their lives during the battle for the liberation of the town in the summer of 1944. And, acknowledging the service to the town by the Irish hospital, Colonel McKinney was a guest of honour at the opening ceremony, together with the American ambassador to France, Douglas Dillon.

The new hospital's first baby, a girl, was born on 26 June 1956. At much the same time, another rite of passage was taking place, as the entire *hôpital irlandais* was transferred into the west wing of the new hospital. In the course of two days some one hundred and forty patients, beds, pharmaceutical supplies, linen, kitchen utensils, and general paraphernalia were transported to the brand-new building on the route de Villedieu at the other end of the town, by a shuttle service of trucks and vans borrowed for the occasion. Some Irish hospital equipment continued to be used for a while after being absorbed into the new building, including Irish-made bandaging equipment which was in use as late as the 1980s. An exhibition at the hospital in April 1996 included many medical and culinary items of Irish manufacture.

By early July 1956, the Irish hospital was reduced to its shell: a set of dilapidated wooden huts, with leaking roofs and peeling paint. They were gradually taken down, and the site was cleared to make space for a *lycée*. A single hut survives to this day, used by the school for indoor sports.

Most of the medical staff returned to Ireland, where they resumed their careers in different hospitals. Jim Gaffney took up an academic appointment in September 1946 as lecturer in clinical pathology in Trinity College Dublin, his alma mater. He was killed in the first Aer Lingus crash in the mountains of North Wales on 10 January 1952. He had been reading a paper at a pathology meeting in Cambridge.

Tim Boland worked in a large maternity department in Sheffield's City General Hospital before taking up a post as an assistant master in the National Maternity Hospital in Dublin. He stood as a Clann na Poblachta candidate for Kildare in the parliamentary elections of January 1948, coming fourth in a three-seater constituency. He died of a coronary in 1954. Patrick Carey, who married one of the Irish hospital nurses, Breda O'Rahelly, worked for a while in England before returning to Dublin's Richmond Hospital where he later specialised in neurosurgery.

Other marriages arising from the Saint-Lô experience included that of George Stewart, the carpenter and buildings superintendent, to Julia Murphy, the nurse-radiographer, Clare Olden, the secretary, to a member of the British forces stationed at Bayeux, Jacqueline de Gromard, a French Red Cross ambulance driver, to Heber McMahon, whom she met while visiting Kitty Sullivan in Dublin, and Freddie McKee to a Saint-Lô woman, Simone Lefèvre. Freddie McKee went to work in the Richmond Hospital. He suffered a fatal heart attack in 1960.

Arthur Darley went back to Saint-Lô in 1947 and visited his Norman friends. On his return he went directly to Our Lady's Hospice in Harold's Cross, Dublin, where he died on 30 December 1948 at the age of forty, of pulmonary tuberculosis. It is not clear whether he had contracted the disease in Saint-Lô while running the tuberculosis ward or in Ireland, prior to going to France. Tommy Dunne wrote to the Théots of Darley's illness: 'I spent a lot of time with him in his last few weeks and we spoke often of the old days at Saint-Lô and of you and your family.' The news of Darley's early death deeply affected Beckett, inspiring a poem entitled *'Mort de A.D.'*.

Not all of the Saint-Lô team died so tragically young. Desmond Leahy returned to England, working as a consultant chest physician in the Birmingham regional hospital board area. On retirement, he studied theology and went to live in Jerusalem, where he still works at the Tantur Ecumenical Institute. Paddy McNicholas left his Tralee ophthalmology and ENT practice early in 1955, to emigrate with his wife and young family to Newfoundland in Canada. He continued to play a role with the Red Cross, and was president of its Newfoundland branch in 1959. After a short time in Zimbabwe he returned to Newfoundland, where he took an active part in politics. Tommy Dunne worked with the Irish Red Cross for a couple of years after returning to Dublin. At first, he wrote to the Théots, he had difficulties re-adjusting after the year and a half spent in France. Dr Kitty Sullivan worked in general practice locums, continuing for a short while after her marriage to a pharmacist, Al Digan. Ned Gumbrielle was attached to Dublin's Cappagh and Temple St Hospitals as an anaesthetist, as well as running a general practice in a north Dublin suburb. Alan Thompson was appointed Professor of Medicine at the Royal College of Surgeons in Ireland in 1962. He died in 1974. Timmy O'Driscoll, the pharmacist, worked for a few years in Ballinasloe, which he described to the Théots as 'a town about the size of Saint-Lô', before moving to London. The hospital's chaplain, Fr Brendan Hynds, worked in the diocese of Ardagh and Clonmacnois, in the parishes of Shrule and later Cloghan, until his retirement in 1988.

Many of the nurses also resumed work in Ireland, although some retired on getting married. Terry Healy nursed at Dr Steevens' Hospital for a brief period, before she married in 1947, while Margaret Malone worked in St Kevin's Hospital

As good as they gave

up to her marriage in 1949. Mary Crowley, the hospital matron, became founder dean of the Faculty of Nursing at the Royal College of Surgeons in Ireland. Nurse Angela Buckley worked in London before moving back to Ireland as matron of a small hospital at the Curragh, Co. Kildare. Kathleen Conroy worked in Peamount Sanatorium in Co. Dublin, Maeve MacDermott was matron at Dublin's Rotunda maternity hospital. Mrs Marguerite Barrett died of leukemia in 1954.

The Irish Red Cross presented each Irish member of staff with a certificate at a ceremony on 30 June 1947. Members of the Irish hospital group met now and then, to drink the health of Saint-Lô and sing *Ma Normandie* or *Nos Vieux Pommiers*. Correspondence from the late 1940s between members of the Irish team and the Théot family reveals enduring attachments. The Irish speak with warm affection for their French friends, expressing nostalgia for Normandy and a longing to be back drinking calvados again. Others besides Arthur Darley made the pilgrimage back to the Manche capital. For example, Michael Killick, the laboratory technician, visited it on his honeymoon, arriving at about 4 a.m. at the Théots' home, where he stayed with his bride. Fifty years later Madame Théot welcomed another Irish visitor, nurse Dilly Fahey, who still remembered *Ma Normandie*.

The years immediately following his Saint-Lô experience marked a highly productive period in Samuel Beckett's literary career, culminating in the sensational success of the first production of *En attendant Godot* (*Waiting for Godot*) in January 1953. From 1946 onwards, Beckett was increasingly to write in French. Many features of Beckett's earlier and later work find resonances in the Saint-Lô experience—humour in response to suffering, human existence pared down to its essentials, a sense of catastrophe combined with notions of redemption. Although one cannot claim that any of these perennial themes derive from his time in the *capitale des ruines,* it is impossible to see the ashbin-dwellers in *Fin de partie* (*Endgame*)

Healing amid the ruins

without recalling the town's inhabitants living in the underground cellars of their ruined houses; and Winnie, in *Happy Days*—buried in a mound of scorched grass, up to her waist in Act One and up to her neck in Act Two—echoes the real experience of a Saint-Lô citizen who was found by rescue-workers standing upright, unable to move, stuck in the ruins of his house. Winnie's care to look her best recalls the women of the town, who would emerge into the sunlight from their dusty cellars, beautifully turned out in starched white blouses. Clov's pursuit of a rat, in *Endgame,* may remind us of the scourge at the hospital, which Beckett had helped to combat by procuring rat poison in Paris.

Beckett's poem 'Saint-Lô', first published in *The Irish Times* on 24 June 1946—and now carved in stone, in a French translation, at the entrance to Saint-Lô's municipal cultural centre—contemplates something much wider and deeper than the river Vire, which is the poem's starting-point. Two pieces he wrote shortly after leaving Saint-Lô reflect his ambivalence towards the Irish hospital project: his talk for Radio Éireann, 'The Capital of the Ruins', dated 10 June 1946, and a poem, entitled 'Antipepsis', dated '1946 After Saint-Lô', first published in 1997 in the Dublin poetry magazine *Metre*. The radio talk was for public consumption—and one critic has even read it as a 'beautiful and moving statement' in which Beckett sets forth some 'articles of faith which will resonate throughout his great works to come'—but the poem 'Antipepsis' is written in another vein. Its jocose opening lines seem to question the rationale of the Irish Red Cross aid project, which had despatched the hospital supplies ahead of its personnel. The planners in No. 21 St Stephens Green Dublin had therefore put the cart before the ass:

> *And the number was uneven*
> *In the green of holy Stephen*
> *Where before the ass the cart*

As good as they gave
Was harnessed for a foreign part.
In this should not be seen the sign
Of hasard, no, but of design,
For of the two, by common consent,
The cart was the more intelligent.

The poem continues in an obliquely mocking tone to depict a world abandoned by reason.

In his biography, James Knowlson points out that the humanitarian side of his work at the Irish hospital brought Beckett out of himself, in a way that his bookish life in the 1920s and 1930s could never have done, and that it introduced him to a wider cross-section of the community than he had previously known. This community was more Irish than French as, ironically, Beckett lived at close quarters with a broader cross-section of Irish people on the Saint-Lô hospital staff than he would have come across previously in the restricted milieux of Foxrock and Trinity College Dublin.

For Beckett, the Saint-Lô experience was a culmination of his experiences in wartime France. It exemplified in a unique way the absurd logic of war. As has been argued by Lois Gordon, the people of Saint-Lô 'illustrated the combination of human misery and human resilience, the absurd victory, that Beckett would shortly write about. The townspeople had achieved liberation through unspeakable suffering.' His postwar writing reflects his response to human suffering, a response imbued with as much compassionate involvement as metaphysical disdain at the absurdity of it all.

French officialdom did not let the Irish hospital staff forget that they had been in Saint-Lô. The chronicle of ceremonies to commemorate and thank them includes the presentation of the *médailles de la Reconnaissance française* at the French Legation in Dublin on 10 April 1948 and Colonel McKinney's reception as guest of honour at the opening of the Mémorial hospital on 10 May 1956. On 27 May 1971, to mark the occasion of the 25th anniversary of the hospital's foundation, a party was held in the French embassy in Dublin, and bronze medals were distributed to the entire surviving staff of Irish personnel. On 7 April 1996, the fiftieth anniversary of the hospital's inauguration, a commemorative ceremony was held in Saint-Lô, attended by Dr Gaffney's widow and the author among other visitors from Ireland, while on 27 October 1998, a delegation from the town presented to the Irish Red Cross Society in Dublin the *livre d'or* of the Irish hospital, a book of testimonies from grateful former patients and their relatives.

Yet, despite these public gestures of gratitude, the idea persists among many people of the town that the Irish have never been adequately thanked for what they did. There is a strange contrast between the series of medals and receptions on the one hand, and the popular perception of official ingratitude on the other hand.

For the Irish, the enterprise was an offer of support to a town in need; they saw it as a duty, and perhaps also as a gesture of gratitude for having escaped the horrors of the war in Europe. But the hospital represented much more than that to the townspeople: for them it symbolised a vote of confidence in the very future of Saint-Lô; they saw the presence of the Irish hospital as a step towards the regeneration of their town. Far more than mere medical aid, the Irish had brought to the *capitale des ruines*, as well as their healing powers and their penicillin, a tangible sense of hope.

The manner in which the help was given was perhaps almost as important as the help itself: the warmth and friendliness, the high spirits—'the nurses were always singing'. 'My mother was regularly treated there,' recalls a French nurse who was born in 1942, 'and she took me with her every time she went. I remember my happiness each time I saw my friends the nurses who were so cheerful and lively and who brought a rare warmth with them. I am now a nurse myself, and I feel

As good as they gave

that the Irish nurses influenced my choice of profession. During those difficult years, we received other kinds of help (postnatal consultations, distribution of food, afternoons when the children were taken to the *don Suisse* (Swiss aid centre) for a shower) but my memories of all this are rather negative. I still have a slight aversion to collective public health. How different it was from the tact, diplomacy and kindness of the Irish hospital staff.'

However, the giving was far from one-way: the members of the Irish Red Cross team brought home with them more than French government medals. In the second half of his talk for Radio Éireann, Beckett shifts from a description of the hospital to a more philosophical tone. He alludes enigmatically to certain intercultural problems between French inhabitants and Irish visitors by concluding that 'their way of being we was not our way and that our way of being they was not their way. It is only fair to say that many of us had never been abroad before.'

Prophesying that the hospital of wooden huts will always be called the Irish hospital, he mentions another possible long-term effect: 'I mean the possibility that some of those who were in Saint-Lô will come home realising that they got at least as good as they gave, that they got indeed what they could hardly give, a vision and sense of a time-honoured conception of humanity in ruins, and perhaps even an inkling of the terms in which our condition is to be thought again. These will have been in France.'

Vire will wind in other shadows
unborn through the bright ways tremble
and the old mind ghost-forsaken
sink into its havoc
Les méandres de la Vire charrieront d'autres ombres
à venir qui vacillent encore dans la lumière des chemins
et le vieux crâne vide de ses spectres
se noiera dans son propre chaos
Samuel Beckett

Saint-Lô, looking across the river Vire towards the place des Alluvions; the old municipal hospital is on the left.
Saint-Lô, vers la place des Alluvions; à gauche, l'ancien hôpital municipal

(Marcel Menant)

A photographic record

The *hôpital irlandais* Saint-Lô
1945–46

Témoignage photographique

Scenes from the old town / Scènes de la vieille ville

'the pleasant and prosperous administrative and agricultural centre that it was'
ce centre administratif et agricole autrefois si agréable et prospère

Samuel Beckett

(above / ci-dessus) The Maison-Dieu, one of the old Norman houses from the Enclos, or oldest centre of the town, within the castle ramparts
La Maison-Dieu, une des vieilles demeures normandes du quartier de l'Enclos, centre vital de la ville médiévale
(Collection Béziers)

(Opposite / ci-contre)
(above / ci-dessus) Rue Torteron/(below / ci-dessous) rue du Neufbourg
two of the town's main streets, running east-west / deux des rues principales est-ouest de la ville
(Robert Pouchin)

(above / ci-dessus*) Rue Carnot/*
(below / ci-dessous*) Place Belle-Croix* (Jean-Pierre Debon)

Scenes that Flaubert or Maupaussant would have recognised at once / Scènes qu'auraient pu reconnaître Flaubert ou Maupassant
(above / ci-dessus) *the open market, place Gambetta* / *le marché sur la place Gambetta*
(below / ci-dessous) *rue Porte-Dollée et rue de Vaux* (Collection Béziers; Jean-Pierre Debon)

(above / ci-dessus) Rues Houssin-Dumanoir et de Villedieu (below / ci-dessous) rue des Noyers

(Robert Pouchin; Jean-Pierre Debon)

During the fighting, summer 1944
Au cours des combats, été 1944

Message urgent

du Commandement Suprême des Forces Expéditionnaires Alliées

AUX HABITANTS DE CETTE VILLE

Afin que l'ennemi commun soit vaincu, les Armées de l'Air Alliées vont attaquer tous les centres de transports ainsi que toutes les voies et moyens de communications vitaux pour l'ennemi.

Des ordres à cet effet ont été donnés.

Vous qui lisez ce tract, vous vous trouvez dans ou près d'un centre essentiel à l'ennemi pour le mouvement de ses troupes et de son matériel. L'objectif vital près duquel vous vous trouvez va être attaqué incessament.

Il faut sans délai vous éloigner, avec votre famille, <u>pendant quelques jours,</u> de la zone de danger où vous vous trouvez.

<u>N'encombrez pas les routes. Dispersez-vous dans la campagne, autant que possible.</u>

PARTEZ SUR LE CHAMP !
VOUS N'AVEZ PAS UNE MINUTE A PERDRE !

Z.F.4

Copy of the leaflet warning civilians to leave the town and spread themselves around the countryside for a few days, dropped by the Allies before the D-Day bombing. Most of these leaflets never reached Saint-Lô, having been blown eastwards by the wind.
Copie du tract lancé par les Alliés avant les bombardements du 6 juin, prévenant les civils qu'ils quittent la ville. Bien de ces tracts tombèrent loin de la ville, emportés vers l'est par le vent.

In the struggle to open the way for the invading forces to pass Saint-Lô, an estimated 11,000 Allied troops and 3,000 Germans lost their lives.
Soldats Alliés, dont 11,000 environ périrent dans les combats, ainsi que 3,000 Allemands.

(Services Américains)

Fighting in the Enclos, the oldest part of the town centre
Le combat dans l'Enclos *(Catherine Lefranc, Services Américains)*

The capital of the ruins / La capitale des ruines

The Bon Sauveur (hospital and school) in ruins / le Bon Sauveur en ruines

(Collection Béziers)

(above) The museum destroyed / (ci-dessus) le musée détruit
(below) Rue des Noyers (how it looked before the bombing see p. 86) / (ci-dessous) Rue des Noyers (avant les bombardements, voir p 86)

(Collection Béziers; Services Américains)

Rue du Rouxelet: The car in the foreground indicates the scale of the destruction.
Rue du Rouxelet: La voiture au premier plan indique l'ampleur des ravages.

(Lavalley)

Two Irish visitors amid the ruins: Dr Jim Gaffney and Martin McNamara, Secretary Irish Red Cross / Deux visiteurs irlandais parmi les ruines: le docteur Jim Gaffney et Martin McNamara, secrétaire de la CRI (*Irish Press* 26 November 1945)

After some of the rubble had been cleared, rue Torteron (see p. 82) looked like this. Rue Torteron, aux débuts du déblaiement (voir p. 82)

(Marcel Menant)

(above) German prisoners clearing away the rubble / (ci-dessus) prisonniers allemands au déblaiement *(below) Life continues, despite the ruins* / (ci-dessous) la vie reprend son cours, malgré les ruines

(Ministère de l'Equipement; Collection Lavalley)

Shell of the bombed municipal hospital (see p. 80)
Ce qui restait de l'hôpital municipal après les bombardements (voir p. 80)

(Marcel Menant)

General de Gaulle's visit to the Capital of the Ruins on the anniversary of the bombing, June 1946
Visite du géneral de Gaulle à la capitale des ruines lors de l'anniversaire des bombardments, juin 1946

(Angela Buckley)

[95]

The Irish Red Cross

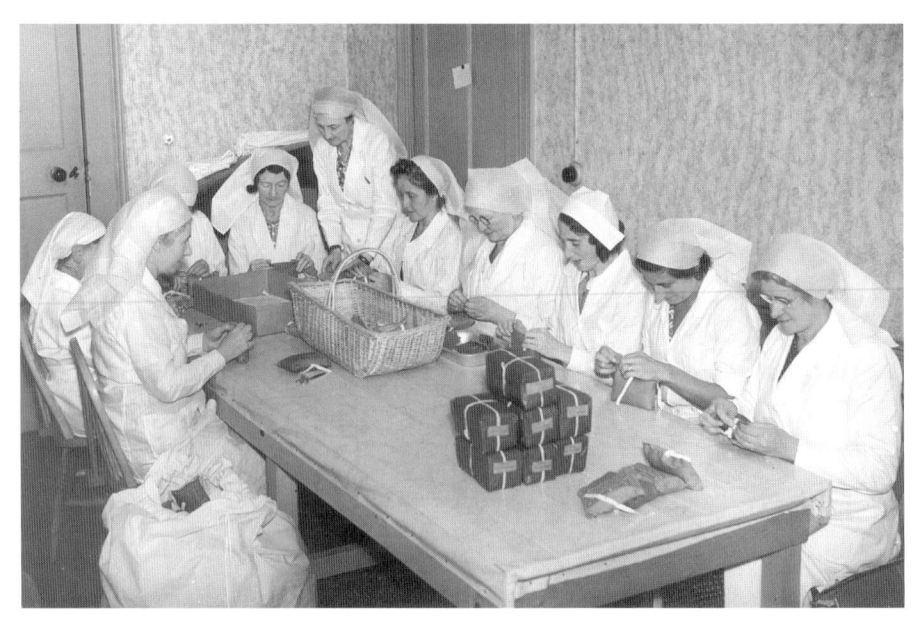

Volunteers in the Irish Red Cross depot, Lincoln Place, Dublin preparing packages for sending abroad/des volontaires de la CRI à Lincoln Place, Dublin, qui préparent le matériel à expédier à l'étranger
(Simone Hale: Irish Press, Irish Times)

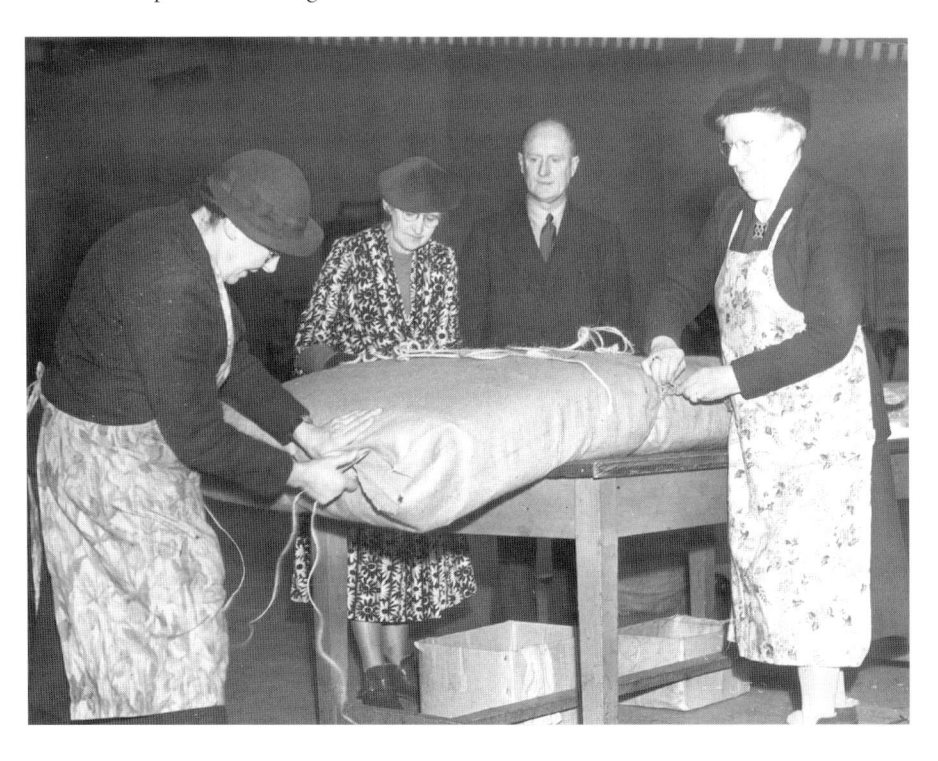

'And the number was uneven
In the green of holy Stephen . . .' Samuel Beckett, 'Antipepsis', 1–2
No. 21, St Stephen's Green, Dublin, former headquarters of the Irish Red Cross Society *(now demolished)* / le no. 21, St Stephen's Green, Dublin, ancien siège de la CRI, aujourd'hui démoli *(Irish Architectural Archive)*

Marguerite Barrett, IRC volunteer, preparing food parcels for Serbian prisoners in Italy.
Emballage d'aide alimentaire pour des prisonniers serbes en Italie. (Simone Hale: Irish Press)

Red Cross Unit For France

("Irish Independent" Special Representative.)

HOSPITAL supplies for the Irish hospital at St. Lo, France, are expected to be sent from Dublin to Granville, nearest shipping point to St. Lo, on or about August 10.

The hospital, which is being staffed and supplied by the Irish Red Cross Society, will serve St. Lo, which had a pre-war population of about 12,000, and the surrounding country within a radius of from 15 to 20 miles.

The supplies will be carried by the motor ship Menapia, owned by the Wexford Steamships Co.. A small party of the Unit will leave a few days earlier to receive the supplies. The remainder will leave between 10 and 14 days afterwards.

FOOD FOR SIX MONTHS.

The supplies, which include hospital and domestic equipment, are valued between £30,000 or £40,000, and sufficient food to keep the hospital supplied for six months will be in the cargo.

Mr. Justice Conor Maguire, Chairman of the Irish Red Cross Society, accompanied by Mr. F. M. Mallin, chemist to the Society, and Miss Crowley, matron of the Unit to France, inspected the supplies, which are housed at the Custom House Quay, Dublin.

Irish Red Cross Hospital Supplies for St. Lo, being inspected by Mr. Justice Conor Maguire and Mr. S. Beckett (interpreter, storekeeper).
—*Irish Independent* Photo (M.).

Samuel Beckett, storekeeper and interpreter: passport photograph, January 1947; Press cutting on hospital supplies, with photograph of Conor Maguire (Chairman Irish Red Cross Society) and Samuel Beckett, inspecting hospital supplies at the port of Dublin Samuel Beckett, intendant et interprète: photo de passeport, janvier 1947; coupure de presse sur l'équipement de l'hôpital, avec photo où figurent Conor Maguire, Président de la CRI, et Samuel Beckett, près d'une des caisses d'approvisionnement, au port de Dublin, avant l'embarquement du matériel pour la France (Irish National Archives; Irish Independent, 31/7/45)

(above) General view of the hospital laid out in wooden huts *(ci-dessus)* vue d'ensemble des baraques de l'hôpital
(centre) Staff photograph, November 1945 / la plupart du personnel, novembre 1945 *(back, left to right / de gauche à droite)* M. Martin, D. Smith, M. Barrett, N. Cunningham, M. Killick, C. Olden, A. Darley, M. Fitzpatrick, A. O'Doherty, M. Fitzgerald, A. M. O'Reilly, T. Dunne, S. Beckett *(front, left to right / de gauche à droite)* F. McKee, J. Murphy, T. Boland, M. Doherty, T. J. McKinney, M. MacDermott, J. Gaffney, E. Mullally, D. Leahy
(left / à gauche) Mary Crowley, Matron / L'infirmière en chef. Her *'impressive matronage was essential to the success of this great enterprise'*—S. Beckett to IRC, 5/2/87

(Angela Buckley; Ethna Gaffney)

(above) Taking time for a smoke on the hospital site / (ci-dessus) *fumant sur le chantier de l'hôpital (left to right* / *de gauche à droite) Freddie McKee, Jim Gaffney, T. J. McKinney, Arthur Darley, Samuel Beckett*
(below) Group at the stud farm, where the hospital supplies were stored, German prisoners behind / (ci-dessous) *groupe au haras, lieu de dépôt du matériel de l'hôpital, en septembre 1945, quelques prisonniers allemands à l'arrière-plan (left to right* / *de gauche à droite) Arthur Darley, French guard with rifle, Samuel Beckett, Freddie McKee, Jim Gaffney, Michael Killick, T. J. McKinney, Tommy Dunne*

(association Shanaghy; Ethna Gaffney, Irish Times 28/9/45)

Poster advertising the official opening of the Irish Hospital, 7 April 1946, carrying side by side the letterhead of the Irish Red Cross Society and the arms of the town of Saint-Lô/ affiche annonçant les cérémonies de l'inauguration officielle de l'hôpital, le 7 avril 1946, portant côte à côte l'en-tête de la CRI en gaélique et l'écusson de la ville de Saint-Lô

(Ethna Gaffney)

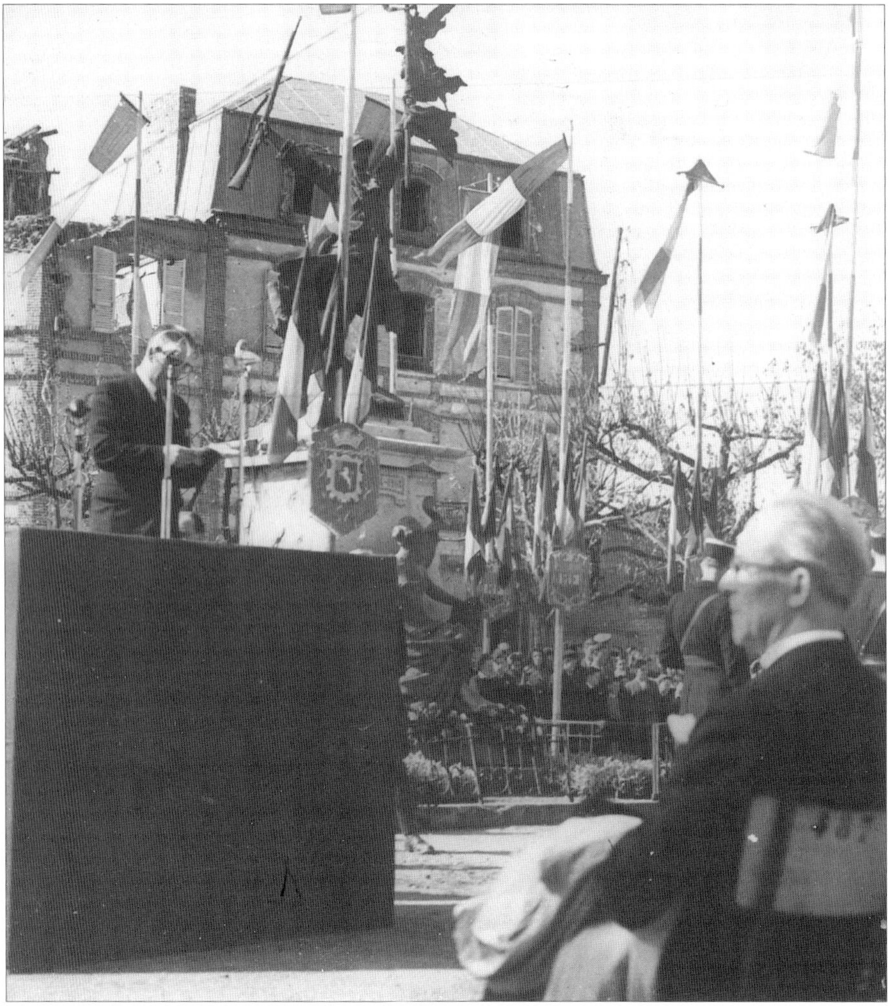

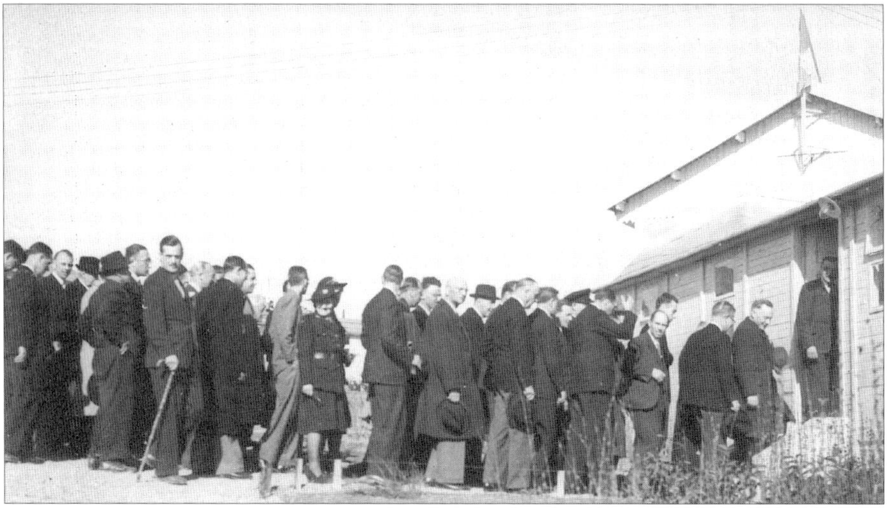

The official opening of the hospital, 7 April 1946: (opposite) speeches, guided tour of the hospital / l'inauguration officielle de l'hôpital, le 7 avril 1946: (ci-contre) discours, visite guidée de l'hôpital *(this page) parade through the rubble-strewn streets, demonstration of thanks* / (cette page) l'inauguration officielle de l'hôpital, le 7 avril 1946: cortège, manifestation de reconnaissance

(Angela Buckley; Desmond Leahy)

Daily life in the hospital / La vie quotidienne à l'hôpital

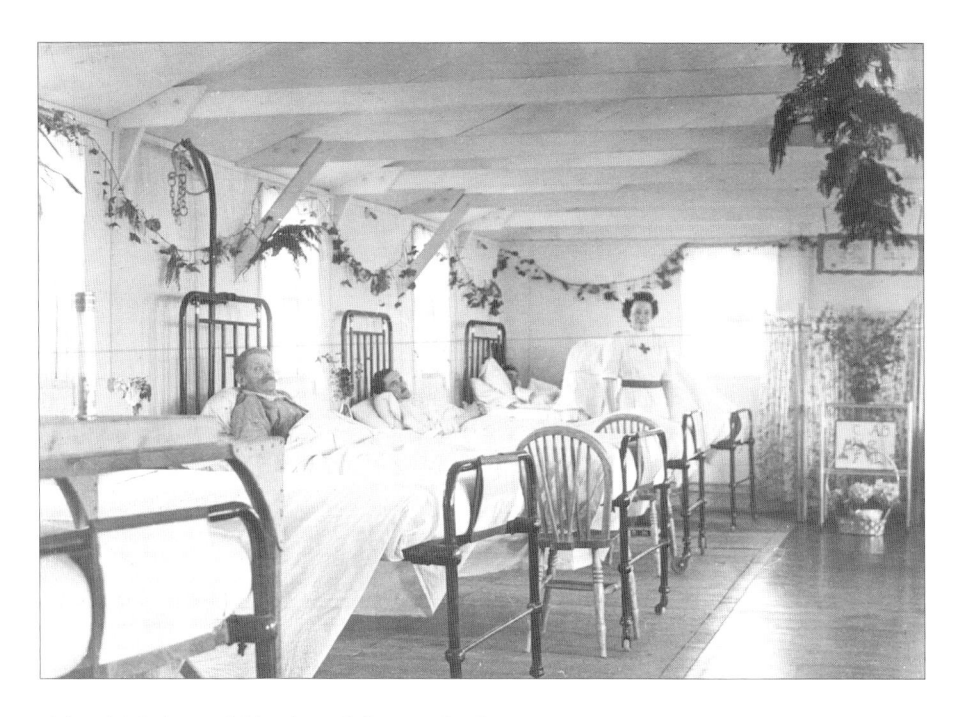

(above) Men's ward / (ci-dessus) l'unité des hommes
(below) Pediatrics ward: nurses Cunningham and O'Driscoll / (ci-dessous) le pavillon de pédiatrie: les infirmières Cunningham et O'Driscoll

(Desmond Leahy; Angela Buckley)

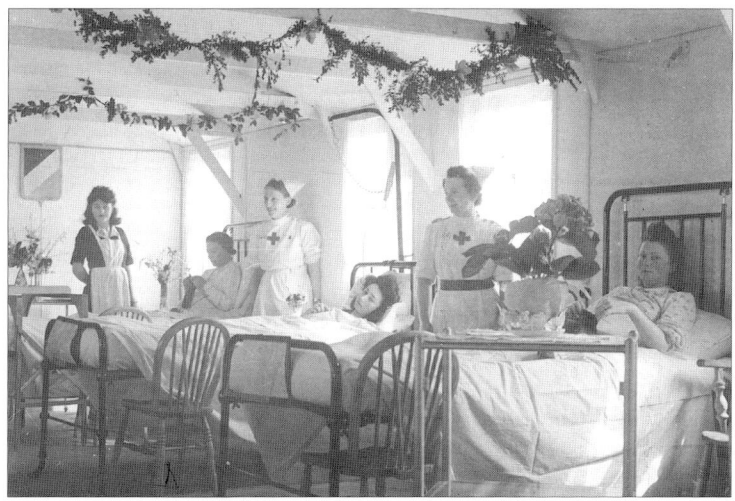

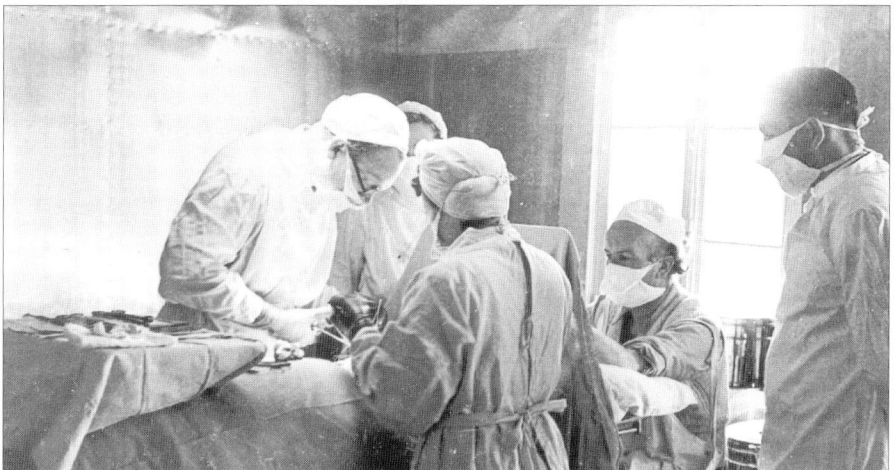

(above) Women's ward / (ci-dessus) l'unité des femmes *(centre)* Operating theatre / (centre) salle d'opération *(below, left* / ci-dessous à gauche) *Some of the child patients cheerfully tucking in* / les enfants à table *(below, right* / ci-dessous à droite) *This unhappy looking child is sufficiently sick to require an oxygen tent* / cet enfant est suffisamment malade pour avoir besoin d'une tente à oxygen.

(Desmond Leahy; Angela Buckley; association Shanaghy)

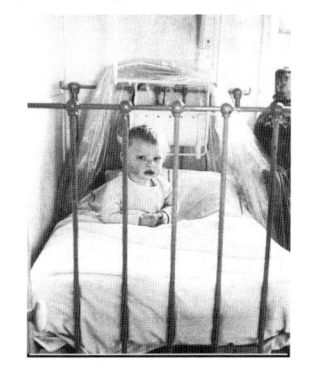

[105]

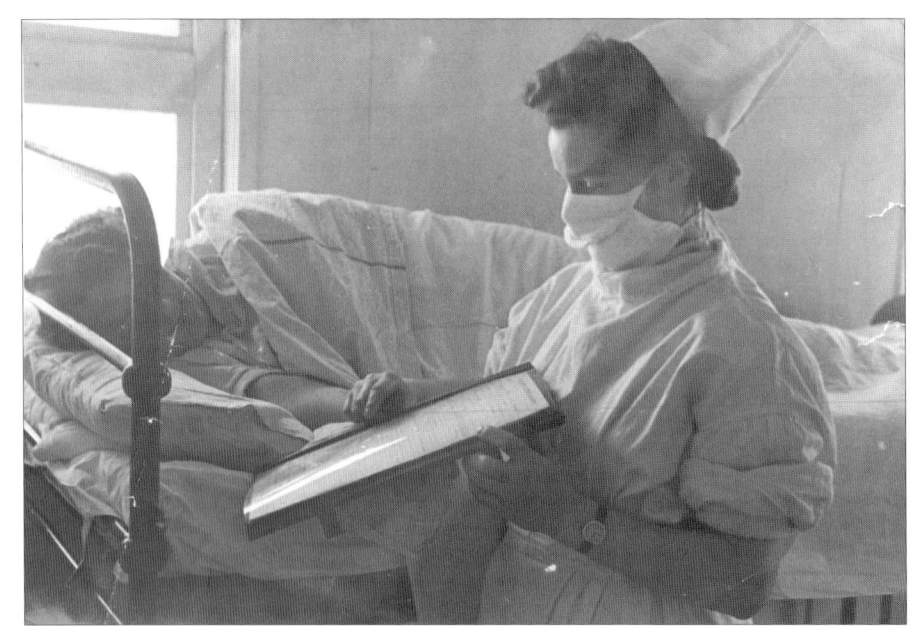

Nurse Dilly Fahey attending a patient / l'infirmière Dilly Fahey soigne un malade

(Kay Kirwan)

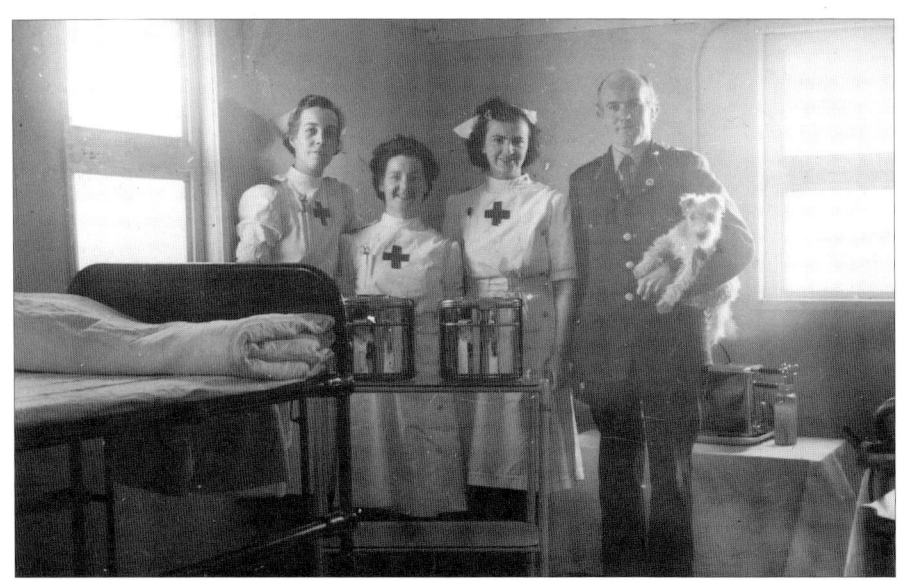

(left to right) Maeve MacDermott, Dilly Fahey, Madeleine Fitzpatrick with Tim Boland and his dog / (de gauche à droite) Maeve MacDermott, Dilly Fahey, Madeleine Fitzpatrick avec Tim Boland et son chien

(Kay Kirwan)

(above) Kitchen with Kathleen Conroy, assistant matron and housekeeper, left, and kitchen staff including German prisoner / (ci-dessus) cuisine, avec à gauche Kathleen Conroy, et du personnel de cuisine comprenant un prisonnier allemand
(below) Hospital chapel, with Fr Hynds, chaplain, saying Mass/ (ci-dessous) la chapelle, où l'aumônier, le père Hynds, dit la messe

(Paulette Villechalane; Desmond Leahy)

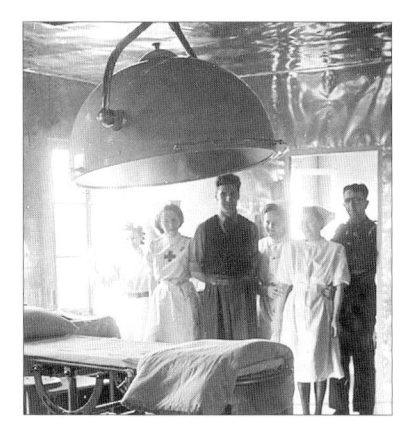

(left) Some of the nurses who arrived in January 1946 / (à gauche) quelques infirmières arrivées en janvier 1946: *Angela Buckley in front, with colleagues Joan Burke, Ann Doherty, Eileen Dunne, Dilly Fahey, Breda O'Rahelly, Madge Trehy (above) The operating theatre lined with aluminium /* (ci-dessus) la salle d'opération aux murs et au plafond tapissés d'aluminium.

(below) Dr Desmond Leahy, Col. McKinney's successor as director, with three members of the administrative staff Agnes O'Doherty, Clare Olden, Dorothy Smith / (ci-dessous) le docteur Desmond Leahy, qui assuma la direction après le retour en Irlande du Col. McKinney, avec quelques membres du personnel administratif *(Angela Buckley; Ethna Gaffney)*

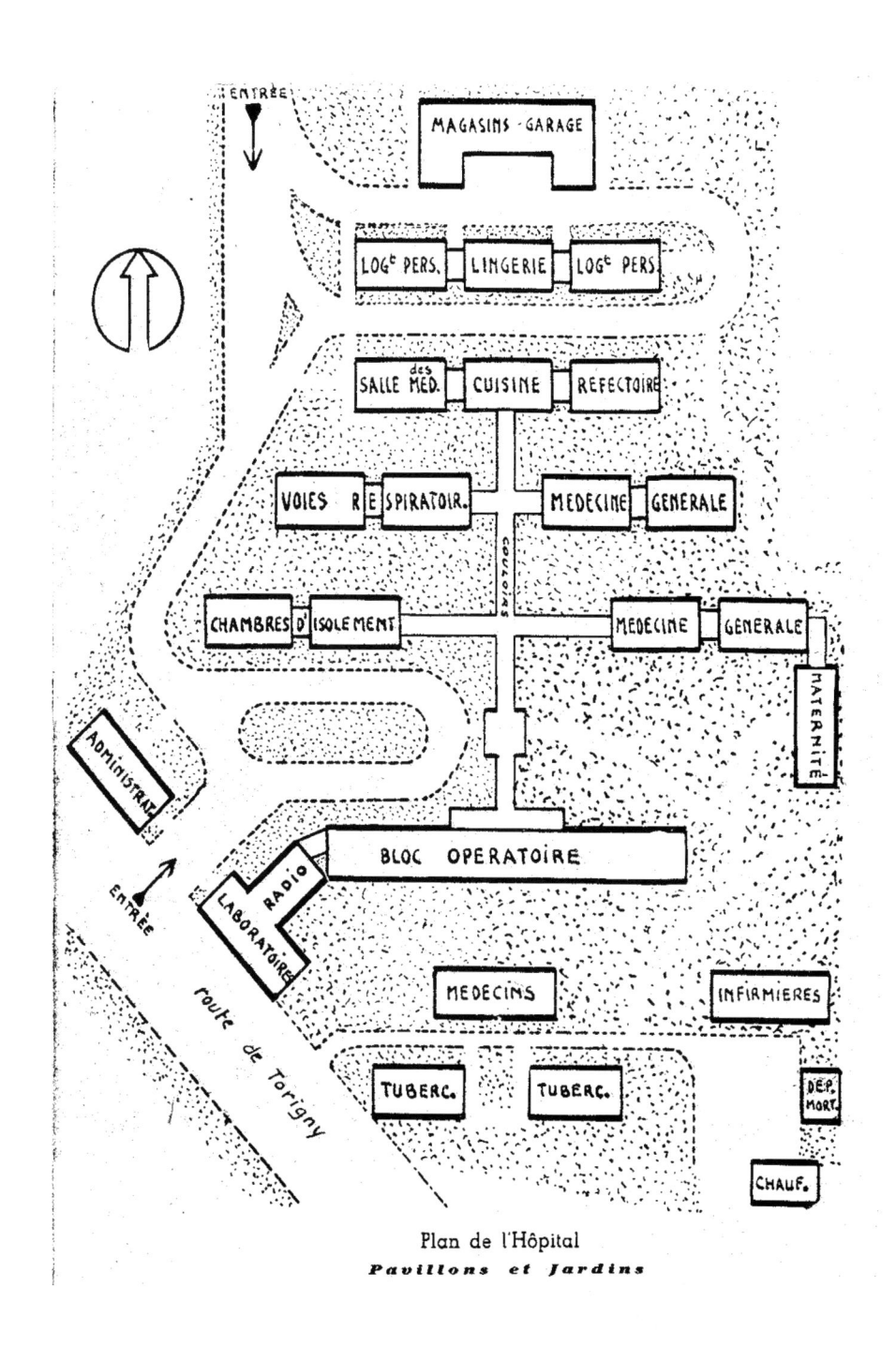

Architect's landscape drawing of the hospital
Plan des baraques de l'hôpital, dessiné par l'architecte Lafont (Ethna Gaffney)

Time off: beyond the ruins / Jours de congé: au-delà des ruines

(left) Cycling round the hospital / (à gauche) promenades en vélo
(right) Vestiges of the battlefield were all around / (à droite) Vestiges du champs de bataille

(below) Relaxing in front of the villa at Coutainville / (ci-dessous) se décontractant devant la villa à Coutainville

(Angela Buckley; Dermot MacDermott)

From Paris to the Pyrenees.... De Paris aux Pyrénées

. . . and back to Saint-Lô / et de retour à Saint-Lô

Franco-Irish gathering at the Café des Ruines, including (2nd & 3rd from right) M. Théot & his son and, in uniform, Timmy O'Driscoll (right) and Tommy Dunne (left) with other French friends/ amitiés franco-irlandaises au Café des Ruines, comprenant, 2e et 3e à droite, M. Théot et son fils avec (en uniforme) Timmy O'Driscoll (à droite) et Tommy Dunne (à gauche) et d'autres amis français

(Angela Buckley; Marie-Anne Théot)

Demonstration to protest against Irish withdrawal, 21 September 1946 / manifestation pour protester contre le départ des Irlandais, le 21 septembre 1946

(Angela Buckley; Desmond Leahy)

Half a century later / un demi-siècle plus tard

(left) Half a century later: hoarding proclaiming the 50th anniversary celebrations, Easter 1996 (right) Jim Gaffney's widow, sister and daughter (the author) at the 50th anniversary celebrations / (à gauche) un demi-siècle plus tard: cinquantenaire de l'inauguration officielle (à droite) la veuve, la sœur et la fille du Dr Gaffney, l'auteur de ce livre, assistent aux cérémonies pour marquer le cinquantenaire

(left to right) Maurice Lerebourg and Cécile Delannoë, two former patients, with Emilie Rouelle and her sister, Marie-Anne Théot, then in her nineties / Maurice Lerebourg and Cécile Delannoë et deux anciens malades, avec Emilie Rouelle et sa soeur, Marie-Anne Théot, nonagénaire

(association Shanaghy)

[113]

L'hôpital des ruines : les Irlandais à Saint-Lô, 1945–46

Saint-Lô 1944: Capitale des ruines

Parmi toutes les villes françaises bombardées lors du débarquement des Alliés en juin 1944, la ville de Saint-Lô fut l'une de celles dont la destruction fut quasi-totale. En effet, dès le lendemain de la bataille de Normandie, la capitale de la Manche fut surnommée "Capitale des ruines", se trouvant presque intégralement ensevelie sous les décombres.

C'est à sa position géographique que la ville devait ce triste sort. Située à la base du Cotentin, au carrefour des axes routiers desservant les plages du débarquement, Saint-Lô fut ciblé par les premiers bombardements aériens alliés le soir du 6 juin, et pendant plusieurs nuits de suite, stratégie cherchant à ralentir, voire empêcher la manœuvre de l'ennemi défendant son territoire occupé.

Les Alliés avaient envisagé de reprendre Saint-Lô aux Allemands le 15 juin, mais il leur fallut plus de quarante jours pour ce faire. Plusieurs facteurs expliquent ce décalage: intempéries, terrain plus propice aux défenseurs qu'aux assaillants, contre-offensive tenace des Allemands. Au cours de la bataille, les troupes alliées subirent d'énormes pertes.

Des centaines de civils périrent également lors des bombardements. Les habitants durent se réfugier là où ils le pouvaient: abris souterrains, caves des domiciles, et dans "le Tunnel", grande grotte souterraine sous les remparts du château qui avait été creusée par les Allemands pendant l'Occupation.

L'hôpital des ruines

Ce tunnel servait de centre d'aide et de traitement des malades et des blessés, service devenu indispensable suite au bombardement de l'hôpital municipal le 8 juin.

Et les bombardements de continuer, sans relâche. Rester ou partir? Comment savoir, au juste, ce qu'il fallait faire? Ceux qui restaient se blotissaient dans leurs refuges. Ceux qui partaient trouvaient à s'héberger dans les fermes des alentours, où s'installaient d'ailleurs des hôpitaux de campagne. Il le fallait bien. Dans les bocages, la vie suivait son cours. Tandis que les uns mouraient, d'autres accouchaient, et les malades se faisaient soigner.

Le 8 juillet, les Allemands ordonnèrent l'exode général des civils. De nouveaux déplacements suivirent pour la population saint-loise, surveillée par les soldats allemands. Moins de trois semaines plus tard, la ville céda enfin aux forces alliées. Après sept semaines de bataille, les habitants allaient regagner leur ville, libérée mais en ruines.

Les dures épreuves qui allaient marquer l'hiver de 1944–45 nous sont connues grâce au témoignage qu'en a fait Louis-Auguste Lefrançois, pharmacien de la ville. Il décrit le lent travail de déblaiement et de reconstruction qui, à peine commencé fin 1944, allait prendre plus d'une décennie. Pendant que la nouvelle ville se redessinait, les habitants vécurent plusieurs années dans des baraques en bois, provenant d'Amérique du Nord et d'autres pays. La préfecture, transférée à Coutances, ne fut rétablie à Saint-Lô qu'en 1953.

Un Conseil municipal provisoire, réuni en octobre 1944, se chargea de la réinstallation des services électriques pour 4000 habitants rentrés chez eux. Il fallait aussi commencer à déblayer les ruines, à enterrer les morts et à restaurer l'eau potable. Le tout sous une pluie constante dans une ville embourbée et infestée de rats. Un témoin décrivit ce qu'il trouva à Saint-Lô — qu'il nomme la "capitale de la catastrophe": «Les habitants de la cité fantôme vivent sous des pans de murs ou dans les caves. Il faut vider les caves avec des seaux, plusieurs fois par

Healing amid the ruins

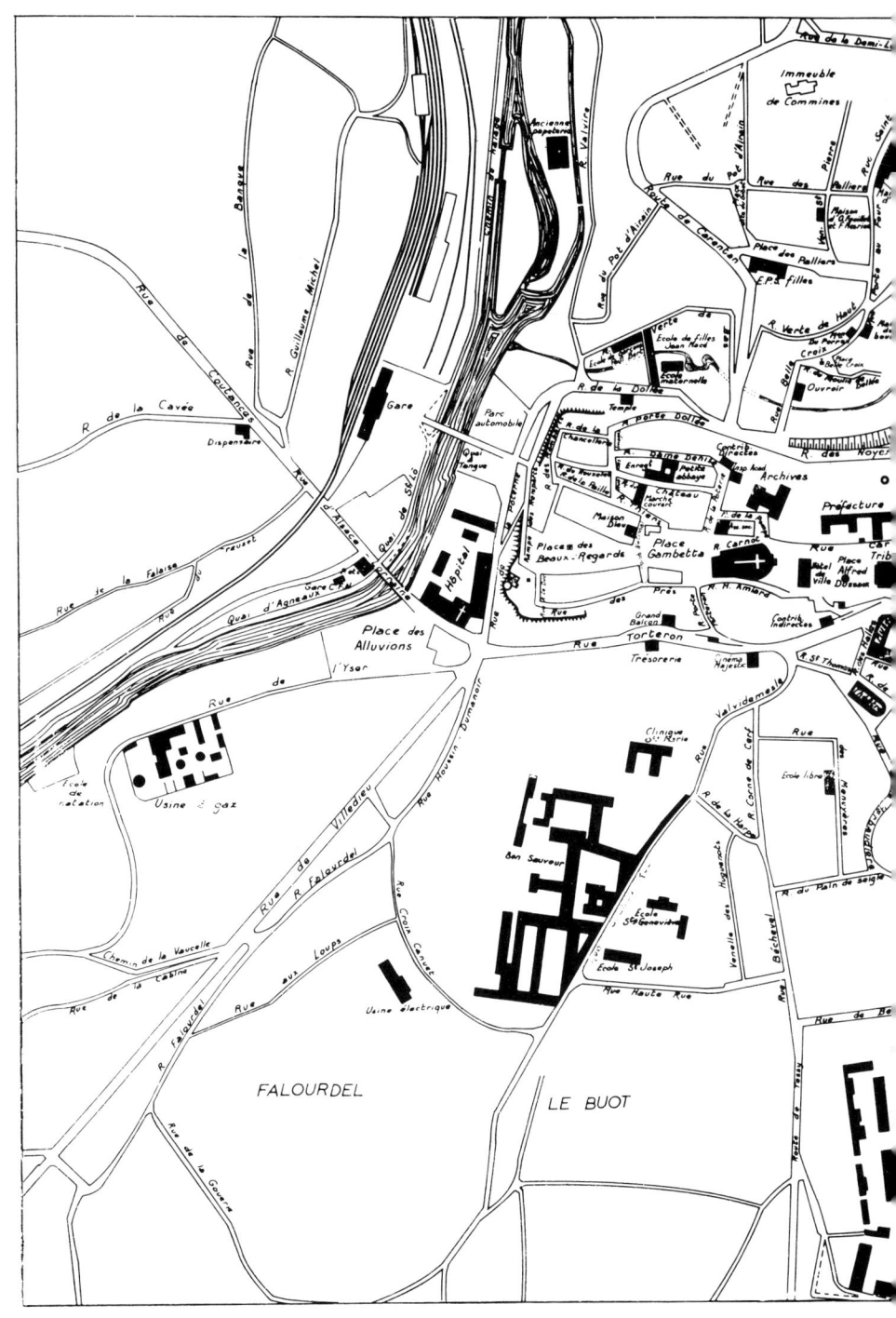

L'hôpital des ruines

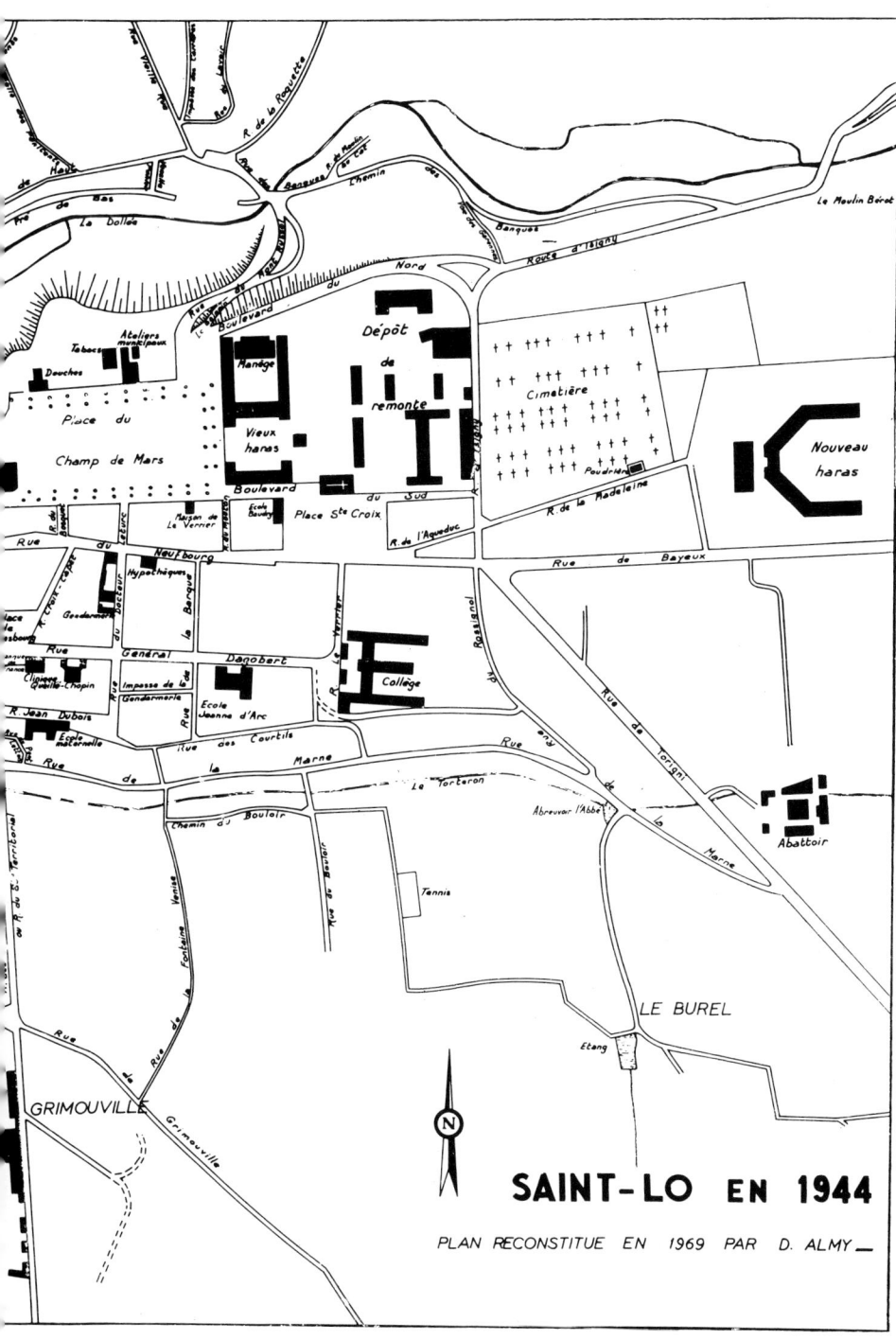

SAINT-LO EN 1944

PLAN RECONSTITUE EN 1969 PAR D. ALMY

nuit [...] Comme l'eau est plus que douteuse, il y a une épidémie de typhoïde naissante; comme il n'y a pas de savon, il y a une épidémie de gale; comme la boue et l'eau s'infiltrent partout, il faut craindre la maladie [...]. C'est à peu près la perfection dans le désastre.» [Jean Éparvier, "J'ai voulu revoir la Normandie... j'ai vu la misère et le dénuement", 1944, sans date précise. A.K. Bell Library, Perth, Archives, dossier PTC 517/9: Saint-Lô Perth Committee]

Quant aux services de santé, les malades durent se soigner dans les villes voisines de Coutances ou de Bayeux; d'autres se rendaient chez le docteur Jean Bourdon ou le docteur Albert Philippe, ancien résistant qui avait survécu au bombardement de la prison en juin 1944. Face à la pénurie de médicaments, ces deux médecins faisaient de leur mieux pour soulager les malades.

Mais ce qui manquait surtout c'était un hôpital. L'hôpital municipal, détruit par les bombardements alliés, avait pu accueillir 500 malades. L'hôpital psychiatrique du Bon Sauveur, détruit lui aussi, survivait dans un seul bâtiment de pierre où on installa après la guerre une clinique d'une cinquantaine de lits. Cet hôpital, quoiqu'admirablement dirigé, ne pouvait pas combler les besoins médicaux de la ville.

L'aide médicale tant requise arriva enfin d'une provenance inattendue. Au printemps de 1945, la Croix-Rouge irlandaise proposa d'établir un hôpital dans les ruines de Saint-Lô. L'offre fut accueillie avec enthousiasme. Mais la genèse de cette proposition d'aide mérite notre attention.

L'offre médicale de la Croix-Rouge irlandaise

La toute jeune Société de la Croix-Rouge irlandaise (CRI), établie en 1939, avait joué un rôle important pendant la guerre — qu'on avait surnommée, dans l'État libre d'Irlande qui demeura neutre pendant le conflit, *the Emergency* ou État d'urgence. Ses 700 divisions avaient co-opéré avec les autorités régionales de l'Etat libre en participant à la préparation des

L'hôpital des ruines

civils pour une invasion éventuelle, qu'elle soit des Alliés ou de l'Axe. Comme leurs homologues en d'autres pays pendant la guerre, les membres de la CRI avaient suivi des cours de secourisme et participé à l'approvisionnement médical. Parmi ses activités, l'organisme menait une campagne anti-tuberculose, dirigeait un centre de don du sang, maintenait près d'une centaine d'ambulances; et son dépôt d'approvisionnement d'urgence aux hôpitaux (*Emergency Hospitals Supply Depot*) à Dublin continua de fonctionner pendant toute la guerre. Outre-mer, la CRI menait des actions d'aide, dont l'envoi d'aide alimentaire et d'autres formes de ravitaillement aux prisonniers de guerre et aux malades des pays combattants d'Europe.

Le financement de ces œuvres de bienfaisance provenait de deux sources: d'une part, des dons volontaires et d'autre part, de la *Irish Hospitals Sweepstake*. Cette agence, tirant des bénéfices provenant de paris hippiques, avait été créée par un homme d'affaires dublinois afin de financer la construction des hôpitaux. Elle avait connu un succès inouï pendant les années trente. Suite à un amendement législatif voté en 1939, la CRI se vit octroyer le droit de gérer pendant la guerre son propre "*sweepstake*", ce qui apporta des crédits considérables à la Société.

Le Conseil de la CRI avait aussi songé à une autre forme d'aide à l'étranger. Au cours de l'été 1943, un Comité s'était réuni régulièrement pour dresser le plan détaillé d'un hôpital de campagne ambulant, qu'ils envisageaient d'envoyer sur le continent européen, afin de soigner les civils blessés pendant la guerre. Ce projet médical ne s'est jamais réalisé, car la CRI s'était heurtée à l'opposition officielle, non seulement à Dublin — où le Ministère de la Défense refusait catégoriquement le détachement du personnel médical de l'Armée irlandaise tant que durerait la guerre — mais aussi à Londres, où le Secrétaire d'État aux Dominions, Lord Cranbourne, avait clairement exprimé son opposition à l'établissement, en zone de guerre, d'un tel hôpital de campagne irlandais.

Malgré cette opposition gouvernementale des deux côtés de

la mer d'Irlande, la CRI ne voulait pas démordre de son projet d'aide médicale à l'Europe. L'année suivante, le 24 août 1944 — veille de la Libération de Paris — le secrétaire de la Société écrivit à Georges Mathieu, secrétaire du Comité de la Croix-Rouge française (CRF) qui siégeait à titre provisoire à Londres, en répétant l'offre d'un centre médical ambulant. Cette offre fut reçue avec enthousiasme, à en juger par deux réponses datées du 31 août 1944, rédigées par Mathieu et par le médecin-général Adolphe Sicé. Celui-ci se déclara touché par la proposition irlandaise, qu'il promit de soumettre au Gouvernement provisoire de la République française ainsi qu'aux autorités alliées, alors que Georges Mathieu évoquait un déplacement à Dublin pour amorcer des discussions.

Entretemps, la CRI redemanda auprès du ministère irlandais de la Défense le détachement d'officiers médicaux militaires au centre médical proposé pour la France; de nouveau la demande fut refusée. Les membres de la CRI insistaient néanmoins sur le détachement d'au moins un individu, le Colonel Thomas McKinney; ils insistèrent tant qu'on finit par accorder le détachement de ce médecin militaire pour une période de six mois. La participation du Colonel McKinney était considérée comme un facteur essentiel au succès de la mission française. Directeur des services sanitaires des forces armées irlandaises, membre actif de la Croix-Rouge irlandaise dès son établissement, McKinney était aussi un linguiste doué, connaissant le français, l'allemand, l'espagnol et le gaélique. Approchant de sa soixantaine, il avait déjà voyagé au nom de la CRI, accompagnant une livraison d'aide à l'Espagne en 1943.

Le projet d'aide offert en 1943 se cristallisait donc, un an plus tard, en un projet d'hôpital d'une centaine de lits, que la CRI allait envoyer quelque part en France. Le recrutement de volontaires se lança au début du mois d'octobre 1944, avec la parution d'annonces dans la presse irlandaise. On cherchait du personnel médical et administratif, pour servir pendant six mois sous contrat renouvelable.

L'hôpital des ruines

La réponse fut encourageante: à la date limite de la réception des candidatures, près de six cents lettres avaient été reçues par la CRI à Dublin. Une quinzaine de médecins furent recrutés avant la fin de 1944, et les infirmières furent interviewées sur quatre jours au début de janvier 1945. Prêts à partir pendant presque douze mois, la plupart des personnes sélectionnées ne devaient se rendre à Saint-Lô qu'à l'automne ou l'hiver suivant.

La réalisation de l'hôpital fut en effet caractérisée par une certaine lenteur, et ce pour plusieurs raisons. La France étant toujours en guerre, les voies normales de communication étaient problématiques. Il fallait commander les uniformes du personnel et rassembler des réserves, en ravitaillement aussi bien qu'en équipement et en médicaments. Et, ce qui n'était certainement pas la moindre des décisions, il fallait déterminer l'emplacement précis de l'hôpital.

Ce dernier objectif justifia l'envoi en France d'un groupe de quatre délégués, mené par le Colonel McKinney, à la fin du mois de mars 1945. Cette équipe d'avant-garde, accompagnée par des représentants de la Croix-Rouge française, parcourut la Bretagne et la Normandie, afin de décider la ville où la CRI devait s'installer. Il s'agissait de choisir entre Brest et Saint-Lô, et la capitale de la Manche fut finalement préférée. Un terrain en pente au bord de la ville ayant été désigné, il fut convenu que les bâtiments — des baraques en bois communiquant par des couloirs — seraient fournis par le Ministère français de la Reconstruction, qui s'occuperait lui aussi de l'installation sanitaire et électrique ainsi que du système de chauffage. La CRI, de sa part, fournirait tout l'équipement et le personnel de l'hôpital, pour une période indéterminée.

De retour en Irlande quelques semaines plus tard, le Colonel McKinney fit appel à la générosité de ses compatriotes. En esquissant l'image de la Normandie dévastée qu'il venait de voir, il déclara que l'on s'attendait à ce que l'Irlande, pays neutre, jouât sa part à la reconstruction tant requise.

La tâche d'approvisionner un hôpital tout entier était

énorme. Il s'agissait de rassembler non seulement le matériel technique des divers services médicaux et chirurgicaux, les produits pharmaceutiques et le mobilier, mais aussi six mois de ravitaillement et d'approvisionnement. Un comité de la CRI, formé à ce seul but, se réunissait toutes les semaines au cours du printemps 1945 pour en organiser l'achat, le stockage et l'emballage. Une équipe de femmes bénévoles travaillait à la fabrication de linge, de draps et de pansements, au dépôt de la CRI à Lincoln Place, à Dublin. En juin, le ministre français à l'Irlande, Jean Rivière, rendit visite à ces dames de la CRI, et les décrivit de cette façon: «À l'étage supérieur, des volontaires dévouées, obligatoirement vêtues de blanc, ourlent les draps, cousent les étiquettes et ne ménagent ni leur habileté, ni leur goût. Pour équiper l'hôpital de cent lits dont la générosité irlandaise veut faire don à la petite ville de Saint-Lô, un matériel considérable est nécessaire qui comprend non seulement les produits pharmaceutiques, les instruments chirurgicaux et tout l'appareil sanitaire moderne, mais encore des réserves de vivres, de linge et même de chaussures. Ce matériel sera prêt à être expédié vers la fin du mois et l'on espère que le transport à destination de la France pourra s'effectuer sans délai.»

Un équipement lourd fut aussi réquisitionné: on décida de transférer en Normandie quelques ambulances de la CRI, ainsi que deux camions, deux groupes électrogènes et un fumigateur. Le tout fut prêt à partir pour la France vers la mi-juillet, et la cargaison entière quitta Dublin pour Cherbourg le 14 août 1945, sur le vaisseau *Menapia*. L'hôpital était finalement en route pour Saint-Lô.

Un hôpital en baraques de bois

Trois Irlandais se trouvèrent au quai de Cherbourg pour surveiller le déchargement de la cargaison: le Colonel McKinney, le docteur Alan Thompson ainsi que Samuel Beckett, qui avait été embauché comme magasinier-interprète. Beckett, qui allait plus tard se faire une renommée mondiale comme auteur d'*En

L'hôpital des ruines

attendant Godot (1953) et lauréat du prix Nobel de littérature en 1969, était relativement inconnu à cette époque. Âgé de trente-neuf ans en 1945, il avait publié quelques essais critiques, un roman et un recueil de nouvelles.

Cet intellectuel irlandais avait fait plusieurs séjours à Paris suite à ses études à l'École Normale Supérieure de 1928 à 1930. Ayant choisi de vivre en France pendant la guerre, il fut actif dans la Résistance à Paris jusqu'à ce qu'il fût obligé de s'enfuir de la Gestapo en août 1942. Il était resté en Provence jusqu'à la fin de la guerre, dans le village de Roussillon d'Apt, avec sa compagne, Suzanne Deschevaux-Dumesnil, qu'il allait plus tard épouser.

C'est au printemps de 1945, lors de son premier retour à Dublin après la guerre, que Beckett avait entendu parler du projet de mise en place d'un hôpital irlandais en France. Son ami, Alan Thompson, lui apprit que la CRI cherchait des personnes parlant couramment le français et qui seraient disponibles pour aller à Saint-Lô. L'idée avait un grand avantage pour Beckett, dans la mesure où cela lui permettrait de rentrer en France comme employé. Il posa sa candidature, fut interviewé par la CRI à la fin de mai, et fut nommé magasinier-interprète à l'hôpital.

La CRI aurait eu du mal à trouver quelqu'un de plus apte au poste. Beckett maîtrisait la langue française et manifestait une sensibilité à l'égard de la culture française. Mais il avait aussi un esprit méticuleux, dont il avait pu faire preuve quelques années auparavant lors de son travail pour la Résistance à Paris. Quoiqu'évidemment très différents, le rôle de magasinier ressemblait en ceci à son travail de résistant, les deux tâches nécessitant le rassemblement et le classement de renseignements détaillés et éventuellement la traduction de ces données avant de les communiquer.

Lors de leur arrivée à Saint-Lô, les trois Irlandais constatèrent que la construction de l'hôpital était moins avancée qu'ils ne l'auraient voulu, cette situation énervant semblerait-il ses deux compagnons beaucoup plus que Beckett. Lui qui avait vécu la guerre connaissait trop bien les énormes problèmes d'ordre pratique qui pouvaient se soulever dans la construction, et ne s'attendait qu'à des délais et des incertitudes dans ce domaine, vu la pénurie matérielle et l'imperfection des voies de communication à cette époque.

En effet, la compréhension de la France qu'avait Beckett le rendait indispensable à l'équipe; une de ses lettres à Thomas MacGreevy, ancien normalien lui aussi, rédigée le 19 août 1945 démontre qu'il était bien sensible, dès le début, à ce qu'il appelle «toutes sortes de tensions obscures entre les médecins du lieu et les gens de la Croix-Rouge à Paris». Commentaire perspicace, qui allait s'avérer tout à fait vrai par la suite, comme nous allons le voir.

Petit à petit, les bâtiments se préparaient néanmoins. Les cinq membres de l'équipe arrivés à Dieppe fin août — le technicien de laboratoire, Michael Killick, le magasinier Tommy Dunne, et les trois médecins, Arthur Darley, spécialiste, Jim Gaffney, pathologiste et Freddie McKee, chirurgien — étaient hébergés tous ensemble (avec les trois premiers arrivés) dans la première baraque prête à les recevoir plus ou moins convenablement. Pendant près de deux mois les huit hommes allaient y dormir, manger, lire, écrire, voire même jouer au bridge ou aux échecs. Ils passaient leurs journées à défaire les caisses d'approvisionnement transportées de Cherbourg et entreposées dans le haras avoisinant. Pour cette tâche ils recevaient l'assistance de quelques prisonniers de guerre allemands contrôlés par Beckett, dont les compétences linguistiques comprenaient la langue allemande.

Et ce fut partout de la boue et de la pluie: un temps très humide rendait difficile le travail de construction et de déchargement. Évidemment, l'uniforme de la CRI n'était pas fait pour ce genre de travail. Le docteur Gaffney, dans une de ses lettres, exprime le souhait d'un bleu de travail et d'une bonne paire de bottes en caoutchouc.

L'hôpital des ruines

Au cours des premières semaines les autres membres du personnel arrivaient également par petits groupes. Il fallait aller à leur rencontre à Dieppe ou à Paris, et Beckett remplissait souvent cette fonction de conducteur. Le docteur Desmond Leahy arriva en septembre, pour remplacer le docteur Thompson; à la mi-octobre ce fut le tour de George Stewart, surveillant de l'entretien des bâtiments, et Maurice Fitzgerald, chargé du transport. Celui-ci, de famille franco-irlandaise et né à Paris, était bilingue; tout comme Marguerite Barrett, réceptionniste, arrivée la semaine suivante avec Clare Olden, secrétaire. Normande de naissance, Marguerite Barrett rentrait en fait chez elle. Née Lefranc, elle avait rencontré son époux irlandais pendant la Grande Guerre lorsqu'elle travaillait comme infirmière de la Croix-Rouge au Havre. En 1939, elle s'était inscrite à la CRI, et avait aidé à la préparation des caisses à Dublin avant de se présenter comme candidate pour la mission de Saint-Lô.

L'arrivée du personnel féminin coïncida avec la mise en marche des installations sanitaires. L'hôpital avait déjà commencé à fonctionner en tant que tel, en septembre, quand le service de consultation fut mis en place. Beaucoup de malades profitaient déjà de la pénicilline apportée de Dublin, produit pharmaceutique peu répandue dans la France de l'après-guerre. Le laboratoire d'analyses du docteur Gaffney, qui devait desservir tout le Département de la Manche, commença à fonctionner en octobre. Les premières infirmières arrivèrent vers le 21 novembre, accompagnées par le docteur Tim Boland, gynécologue-obstétricien, et Dorothy Smith, qui allait travailler dans l'administration. Au mois de décembre, la construction terminée, on pouvait enfin accueillir des malades et les hospitaliser.

L'hôpital avait finalement triomphé du chaos et de la boue des premières semaines. Le témoignage du journaliste Albert Desile est à propos. Rédigé en décembre, et imprimé dans le Bulletin de la CRI en janvier 1946, l'article raconte sa visite au site, composé de «25 baraquements blancs comme neige et garnis intérieurement 'd'isorel' immaculé qui leur donne un aspect sympathique et confortable.» Il décrit un espace ordonné et propre: «La cuisine [...] communique avec le Pavillon de la Médecine Générale relié lui-même par de longs couloirs avec les pavillons réservés à la maternité, à la tuberculose, aux chambres d'isolement et à la chirurgie. Le dispensaire, le laboratoire définitif, la salle de radiographie, la morgue, les locaux destinés aux services administratifs sont eux aussi en voie d'achèvement. La lingerie, les dortoirs, la salle à manger réservés au personnel médical sont coquettement parés et fleuris depuis la venue de Miss Olden et de ses compagnes.»

Juste avant Noël, un télégramme de Dublin annonça une triste nouvelle: Róisín McKinney, la femme du directeur, était gravement malade. Beckett accompagna le Colonel à Paris, mais il arriva en Irlande trop tard pour revoir son épouse vivante. Pendant son absence, le docteur Gaffney agissait comme directeur adjoint.

L'infirmière en chef, Mary Frances Crowley, arriva par temps de neige la veille de Noël. Beckett la conduisit de Dieppe à Saint-Lô, où elle se rendit immédiatement à l'église de Notre-Dame pour assister à la messe de minuit. Un deuxième groupe d'infirmières quitta Dublin le 5 janvier, ainsi que l'anesthésiste, le docteur Edward Gumbrielle, l'ophtalmologue, le docteur Paddy McNicholas, et le pharmacien, Tim O'Driscoll. C'est également en janvier 1946 qu'arriva l'aumônier de l'hôpital, le père Brendan Hynds. Ce prêtre irlandais avait fait une année d'études au Collège des Irlandais dans le Quartier latin à Paris, et comme il avait travaillé pendant quatre ans dans une paroisse à Gennevilliers, dans la banlieue nord de la capitale, il ne se sentait pas trop dépaysé, et parlait couramment le français.

Mais ce n'était pas que du personnel qui arriva au mois de janvier: la Maternité accueillit son premier bébé qu'on appela Patrick Noël. Au cours du printemps le personnel devenait de plus en plus occupé. On demanda des volontaires supplémentaires: un deuxième technicien de laboratoire, Roderick Murphy, un deuxième chirurgien, le docteur Paddy Carey, ainsi que la docteur Kitty Sullivan, généraliste, arrivèrent au printemps. Celle-ci travaillait avec le docteur Darley au service de consultation, où les queues se formaient dès 6 heures du matin. Au début du mois d'avril près d'une centaine de malades hospitalisés étaient soignés.

Le 7 avril 1946, les cérémonies fêtant l'inauguration officielle de l'hôpital allaient durer près de dix-huit heures, à en juger des divers récits écrits, publics et privés, qui ont survécu à l'événement. Étaient présents des représentants des deux gouvernements, de la CRF et la CRI; dans les rues en ruines parées des deux tricolores, des foules manifestaient leur reconnaissance aux Irlandais, et l'orchestre de la Flotte joua l'hymne national des deux républiques. Le maire accueillit plus d'une centaine d'invités à un déjeuner; un cortège déposa une gerbe au monument aux morts; et après une série de discours — prononcés par le maire, Georges Lavalley, le président de la CRF et le président de la CRI, le ministre d'Irlande en France, Seán Murphy et le sous-secrétaire d'Etat à la Population, Pierre Pflimlin — un concert, un grand bal et une séance de chansons à l'hôpital se prolongèrent tard dans la nuit.

Après cette longue journée de festin empreinte d'émotions vivement ressenties, l'hôpital irlandais faisait incontestablement partie de la ville de Saint-Lô. Les membres de la CRI, visitant la ville en ruines pour les cérémonies d'avril, s'exprimaient bien fiers de la réalisation de leur œuvre. Et les commentateurs français de même. Tel le rédacteur d'un article pour la revue *France Croix-Rouge* paru en juin 1946 ("La Croix-Rouge Irlandaise offre un Hôpital à la Croix-Rouge Française", *France Croix-Rouge*, juin 1946, p. 3), qui en donne une description détaillée et positive: «On vient d'inaugurer à Saint-Lô, dans la Manche, un hôpital offert par la Croix-Rouge irlandaise à la Croix-Rouge française. Cet hôpital de cent lits, entièrement équipé par l'Irlande et fonctionnant avec un personnel irlandais, rend d'inappréciables services dans une région entièrement dévastée, l'une des plus éprouvées de France. [...]

«Quoique construit en baraques de bois, l'hôpital de Saint-Lô répond à tous les besoins qu'il est appelé à rendre: groupées d'une manière harmonieuse au milieu d'un vaste emplacement ensoleillé, elles comprennent: un service médical de 40 lits, une maternité de 20 lits très complète, un pavillon pour enfants de 10 lits, un bloc opératoire impeccable avec salles d'hospitalisation, 30 lits, des cabinets de consultation avec radios, laboratoires et pharmacie, un secrétariat et un service de renseignements. Le personnel est logé dans des pavillons spéciaux où des foyers sont aménagés pour leurs loisirs; enfin une vaste baraque abrite les réfectoires et les cuisines. Il faut aussi mentionner la chapelle, la lingerie, les garages et dépôts et la chaufferie.

«L'hôpital de Saint-Lô est géré par le Dr irlandais MacKinney. Tous ses assistants et tout son personnel ont abandonné volontairement leur famille, leur foyer et leur clientèle, pour se consacrer à cette œuvre. Le fonctionnement de l'hôpital est assuré aux frais de la Croix-Rouge irlandaise. [...] Ce don mérite toutes les reconnaissances car il n'est pas seulement un fait matériel mais il représente une somme de dévouement et de sacrifices quotidiens qu'il n'est pas possible de chiffrer puisqu'elle est infinie.»

L'hôpital s'était vite fait une renommée exceptionnelle, comme en témoigne un habitant de la ville, Raymond Lelièvre: «Les salles se remplissent très vite et devant l'accueil qui leur est fait (les Irlandais reçoivent avec bonne grâce) les défilés aux consultations s'épaississent chaque jour, on y retrouve des figures et des silhouettes dignes de la cour des Miracles. [...] L'Hôpital ne reçoit pas avec bienveillance que les malades, il reçoit aussi les curieux dans mon genre, et c'est en trinquant au Whisky, le 'Calva' de l'Irlande, que j'ai fait connaissance avec cet admirable peuple qui nous a adoptés, et qu'à notre tour nous adoptons avec joie et reconnaissance en nos murs

L'hôpital des ruines

[...] qui ne sont plus.» [*Terre Normande*, mars/avril 1946, p. 14]

Les malades, provenant parfois de très loin, se trouvaient en général bien contents des soins reçus gratuitement. Un des atouts de l'hôpital était sans doute l'abondance de la pénicilline importée d'Irlande, médicament alors rarement disponible pour les civils. Ceux-ci, accoutumés pendant la guerre à un régime alimentaire mal équilibré, souffraient de la gale et d'autres maladies de la peau. Un pavillon recevait les tuberculeux, dont la majorité était des hommes rentrés du STO ou des camps de concentration. Un médecin de la ville spécialiste dans ce domaine, le docteur Jean Bourdon, travaillait dans cette unité.

Le service des Urgences était constamment sollicité, recevant les accidentés résultant des mines non explosées qui parsemaient les campagnes des alentours, ou bien les victimes d'écroulements de maçonnerie bombardée. D'autres accidents relevaient plutôt des accidents typiques en temps de guerre ou de paix qui arrivent aux enfants: ainsi le petit Maurice Lerebourg, âgé de huit ans qui, s'étant renversé un récipient d'eau bouillante, fut hospitalisé pendant six mois et dut subir une série de greffes de la peau.

La Maternité comprenait vingt-quatre lits, deux salles d'accouchement et une unité spéciale consacrée aux prématurés. Ce service était particulièrement apprécié des femmes qui, pour la première fois depuis des mois, pouvaient accoucher en sécurité, dans une ambiance propre et chaleureuse. L'hôpital maintenait aussi un centre prénatal et postnatal et son service de pédiatrie était également très fréquenté.

Il paraît qu'on mangeait bien à l'hôpital; les produits régionaux étaient d'une excellente qualité, et malgré les rationnements de la viande et du beurre, le régime alimentaire était varié et suffisant. Les Irlandais complétaient d'approvisionnements frais normands leurs réserves d'aliments apportés de Dublin.

On pouvait entendre une diversité de langues à l'hôpital: en plus de l'anglais et du français, l'allemand, l'espagnol, le

Healing amid the ruins

breton, l'arabe et le gaélique étaient utilisés; quelques Polonais et un Italien faisaient eux aussi partie de l'équipe. Treize prisonniers de guerre allemands aidaient à la préparation des repas et à l'entretien des locaux.

Ainsi, ayant débuté comme un chantier boueux jonché de baraques à moitié terminées, le projet de la Croix-Rouge irlandaise s'était transformé en quelques mois en un hôpital bien efficace et très apprécié. Peut-être sa réussite se devait-elle à une formule unique qui mariait la bonne volonté et les dons des diverses nationalités qui participaient à sa réalisation. Un architecte français ayant bien réfléchi à l'exploitation rationnelle du site et des bâtiments; un cuisinier français auquel ne manquaient ni produits frais régionaux ni aide à son travail; un groupe de jeunes soldats allemands dont la tâche était de veiller à la propreté impeccable des locaux; et enfin, une équipe de médecins et d'infirmières irlandais, faisant preuve d'une chaleur humaine et d'un professionnalisme exemplaires.

En effet, cet hôpital irlandais semble avoir beaucoup marqué ceux qui y furent guéris. D'une part, on était impressionné par la qualité des soins reçus et, d'autre part, par le fait que ce traitement avait été offert à titre gratuit. Les patients témoignaient de leur reconnaissance de plusieurs manières: par des dons d'aliments, de fleurs, de bouteilles de calvados, par des invitations personnelles. Les anciens malades se disaient surtout reconnaissants aux infirmières, dont le dévouement et la vocation à leur travail semblaient vraiment exceptionnels.

Dans un texte sur Saint-Lô rédigé pour la radio irlandaise en juin 1946, Samuel Beckett parle d'une autre facette de l'hôpital irlandais: il constate que toute l'aventure de la CRI dépendait des rapports établis dès le début entre Irlandais et Saint-Lois, rapports sociaux bien plus importants que la seule relation entre médecins et malades. C'est vers cet autre domaine, celui des contacts humains au-delà du lieu de travail, que nous aimerions tourner notre regard.

L'hôpital des ruines

Au-delà du rapport thérapeutique

Dès leur arrivée, les Irlandais s'intégrèrent rapidement à la population saint-loise, et finirent par nouer tout un réseau de rapports avec divers groupes dans la ville et ses alentours en 1945–46.

Aussi, pendant leur temps libre fréquentaient-ils les courses de chevaux, concerts et bals organisés dans la région. Certains d'entre eux empruntaient les chevaux au haras pour monter à cheval. On les invitait aux mariages, ils assistaient aux obsèques; des enfants venaient jouer dans le parc de l'hôpital; on y servait le thé le dimanche après-midi. Le maire, Georges Lavalley, fut très apprécié du personnel. Lors de la mort de la femme du Colonel McKinney, une messe fut célébrée dans la paroisse locale. La différence linguistique ne posait pas de problèmes entre les Saint-Lois et les Irlandais qui parlaient imparfaitement leur langue. Une Saint-Loise qui avait l'habitude de recevoir les visiteurs témoigna d'une soirée de Noël où l'on chanta en chœur l'*Adeste Fideles* en latin.

Un des rendez-vous favoris des Irlandais fut le Café des Ruines, au centre de Saint-Lô, géré par Monsieur et Madame Théot. Ceux-ci étaient rentrés de l'exode en février 1945 pour trouver leur maison en ruines, mais ils avaient improvisé un nouveau café-restaurant dans les décombres d'un autre bâtiment. Marie-Anne Théot, aujourd'hui nonagénaire, rappelle leurs difficultés à aménager ce local, sans toit ni fenêtres. C'est dans ce café parmi les ruines qu'elle et son mari recevaient les bénévoles irlandais, qui s'y rendaient régulièrement en tant qu'invités de la maison, pour manger et boire tout leur content. L'amitié ainsi nouée persista par correspondance bien après le départ des visiteurs.

Du moment qu'ils parlaient anglais, la langue des Alliés, les membres de la CRI de Saint-Lô pouvaient prendre contact avec les divers groupes de personnel anglophone déployé en Normandie après la guerre. Ils avaient des relations excellentes avec les camps américains et britanniques dans la région, relations qui se traduisaient par une coopération à plusieurs niveaux: prêt d'un véhicule militaire britannique à long terme; don de meubles et de matériel dont les Américains n'avaient plus besoin; services d'un aumônier américain avant l'arrivée du père Hynds; invitations réciproques aux dîners et aux soirées; échanges de soins médicaux pour des litres d'essence. Comme il est souvent le cas, les militaires américains finissaient souvent par avoir des ancêtres originaires de l'île d'Émeraude.

À l'hôpital, une des baraques fut réservée aux loisirs du personnel. On y jouait au pingpong, on y organisait des fêtes. De grands bals s'y tenaient, à Noël, à mardi gras, à la Saint Patrick — le 17 mars 1946. En effet, les Irlandais savaient bien s'amuser — une réputation nationale sans doute agrandie par les circonstances d'un groupe de personnes, célibataires et relativement jeunes pour la plupart, se trouvant à l'étranger pour la première fois. Ni le cidre, ni le vin, ni le calvados ne manquaient en Normandie à cette époque . . .

La Croix-Rouge française était également en contact avec les Irlandais, aussi bien à Paris quand ils s'y rendaient pour des réunions officielles, que sur Saint-Lô, où ils avaient des rapports avec le comité départemental. Le comte de Kergorlay, du château de Canisy, avait hébergé les premiers des Irlandais arrivés de Dublin en août 1945, et au printemps suivant il fit don à l'hôpital de sa résidence secondaire à Agon-Coutainville. Cette propriété au bord de la mer, entourée d'un jardin avec massifs, arbres et pelouses, pouvait héberger dix-sept personnes. Elle avait été réquisitionnée pour servir de clinique pendant la guerre. La CRI la loua à partir du mois de mai 1946 comme maison de repos pour son personnel et pour servir de lieu de convalescence. Médecins, infirmières et autres membres du personnel ont tous profité de cette retraite côtière pendant leurs weekends de congés au cours des mois chauds de l'été. La villa était entretenue par une certaine Madame Pilorget, ancienne infirmière dont l'excellente cuisine était très appréciée.

Certains congés furent passés plus loin: on montait à Paris,

L'hôpital des ruines

on visitait Bayeux ou Lisieux. De temps à autre on faisait des excursions plus lointaines. Bien des Irlandais se rendaient à Lourdes; quelques-uns traversaient la frontière jusqu'en Espagne, en Italie ou en Suisse.

Les témoignages d'anciens malades de Saint-Lô, recueillis autour de la ville de 1996 à 1998 par l'association Shanaghy, sont tous extrêmement positifs sur les rapports entre les Irlandais et les citadins qu'ils servaient. Le contexte de l'après-guerre y joua certainement un rôle. La reconstruction, époque de co-opération et d'entraide, était une période où il était relativement facile de nouer des rapports affectifs avec des étrangers. En commentant sur l'esprit de camaraderie de l'époque, David Desramé, auteur d'une thèse sur la reconstruction de Saint-Lô, suggère que la nature provisoire des baraques de l'hôpital irlandais était importante à cet égard. Il cite une sage-femme qui, ayant travaillé à l'hôpital irlandais avant de déménager au nouvel hôpital du Mémorial, dit qu'elle préférait l'ambiance des baraques en bois au bâtiment permanent qui les remplaça par la suite. Selon son témoignage, l'esprit de famille se ressentissait plus intensément à l'hôpital irlandais.

Il ne faut pas non plus oublier que la présence des Irlandais à Saint-Lô coïncidait avec la Libération. Les anciens malades évoquent les bals et les soirées à l'hôpital, et les séances de musique avec le docteur Darley au violon et le «grand Sam» (Beckett) au piano. Une joie de vivre y régnait: bien des témoignages constatent que les infirmières ne cessaient de chanter.

La reconnaissance des citadins fut exprimée de manière officielle. En juin 1946, on annonça aux bénévoles irlandais que le Gouvernement provisoire allait leur accorder individuellement la médaille de la Reconnaissance française. Mais, comme le constate Samuel Beckett dans son texte rédigé la même année pour la radio irlandaise, les Irlandais profitèrent de bien plus qu'une médaille. Ils rapportèrent sans doute chez eux quelque chose de bien plus significatif, à savoir un sentiment renouvelé de la condition humaine, fourni par ce que Beckett appela «l'humanité en ruines» qu'ils avaient découverte à Saint-Lô.

L'affaire de l'hôpital irlandais

La durée précise de la mission française de la Croix-Rouge irlandaise n'avait jamais été très claire, et au cours de l'été et de l'automne 1946, cette question devint un problème de plus en plus critique. En effet, pendant plusieurs semaines, le personnel de l'hôpital baignait dans l'incertitude, incertitude d'autant plus aggravée par trois facteurs.

D'une part, la CRI considérait sérieusement la possibilité d'établir en Pologne un hôpital pareil à celui de Saint-Lô. En juin 1946, elle avait envoyé deux délégués à Varsovie pour en discuter avec les autorités polonaises. On parlait de ce projet dans la presse irlandaise; et quelques médecins et infirmières postés en Normandie songeaient à se déplacer dans ce nouvel établissement. Finalement, pour une gamme de raisons complexes, ce projet d'hôpital en Europe de l'est ne s'est jamais réalisé.

Un autre facteur semant l'incertitude à l'hôpital fut sans doute celui de la question du remplacement du directeur. Le Colonel McKinney ayant été réintégré à l'Armée irlandaise en mai, le docteur Desmond Leahy dirigeait l'hôpital, jusqu'à sa nomination officielle comme directeur vers la fin du mois de juillet. Pendant près de trois mois, on ne savait qui allait être nommé, ni quand, ni pour combien de temps.

Une troisième source d'incertitude — et ce ne fut certainement pas la moindre — était d'ordre financier. La situation financière de la Croix-Rouge irlandaise était devenue critique au printemps de 1946. L'hôpital de Saint-Lô lui avait déjà coûté £40,000, et les frais d'entretien et d'équipement s'estimaient d'un montant avoisinant les £50,000 pour six mois, tandis que le personnel coûtait entre mille et deux mille livres par mois. La Société avait d'autres activités à diriger en Irlande,

L'hôpital des ruines

telle la campagne de lutte contre la tuberculose, maladie particulièrement répandue en Irlande à l'époque.

En plus, pour aggraver la situation financière de la CRI, celle-ci n'avait plus le droit de recueillir des fonds par le biais des *Sweepstakes*. Une fois la guerre finie, la législation de 1939 qui avait permis à la CRI cette forme de collecte de fonds cessa d'être en vigueur — malgré des tentatives de la part de la Société de contester la nouvelle situation législative.

Ainsi, le statut particulier dont jouissait la Société pendant la guerre s'arrêta au moment même où ses besoins financiers se faisaient le plus sentir, lors de la réalisation du projet médical à Saint-Lô. Il semblait donc inévitable que les Irlandais soient obligés de quitter leur hôpital des ruines. Cependant, la manière dont ils prirent congé de Saint-Lô suscita diverses tensions, et pendant les mois de l'automne ils se trouvèrent au centre d'un scandale municipal, la soi-disant «Affaire de l'hôpital irlandais». Les tensions découlaient des attitudes différentes manifestées à l'égard de l'hôpital par les autorités municipales, la Croix-Rouge française et les médecins français.

Qu'il y ait conflit d'intérêt entre leur travail d'aide humanitaire et le gagne-pain des médecins de la ville avait été bien reconnu par les médecins irlandais. Ce conflit éventuel est mentionné par le docteur Gaffney, déjà au début de leur séjour, dans sa correspondance du mois d'août 1945, et par Samuel Beckett, qui note bien les deux pôles du problème dans une lettre rédigée le même mois. Beckett observe que le personnel médical indigène souhaitait bien recevoir le matériel de Dublin, mais pas le personnel; il ajoute par contre que la Croix-Rouge française insistait à ce qu'on envoie une équipe irlandaise aussi. Néanmoins, les deux groupes de médecins étaient arrivés à une coopération plus ou moins fructueuse. Le docteur Bourdon dirigeait par exemple la salle de traitement de la tuberculose; une sage-femme française était invitée à travailler avec le docteur Boland dans la salle d'accouchement; et sur le plan des amitiés, les rapports étaient apparemment cordiaux,

Healing amid the ruins

les docteurs français et irlandais jouant au bridge et dînant ensemble.

Pourtant, au fil des mois, le besoin des médecins saint-lois de retrouver leur situation professionnelle de l'avant-guerre se faisait de plus en plus ressentir. Finalement les événements allaient se dérouler d'une manière imprévue, de façon à les embarrasser au maximum.

D'abord, le 3 août 1946, les docteurs Gaffney et Leahy informèrent le maire de la ville, Georges Lavalley, que la Croix-Rouge irlandaise venait d'annoncer sa décision de transférer la gestion de l'hôpital irlandais à la Croix-Rouge française le 31 octobre. Cela entraînerait le départ des Irlandais à la même date. Quand Lavalley transmit cette nouvelle au Conseil municipal du 5 août, les conseillers lui demandèrent de faire de son mieux pour essayer de persuader la CRI de réviser sa décision, afin de permettre aux Saint-Lois de profiter de la présence des Irlandais au moins jusqu'en octobre 1947. Le maire rendit visite par la suite au ministre d'Irlande, Seán Murphy, à Paris et on écrivit au Premier ministre irlandais, Éamon de Valera, qui fonctionnait en même temps comme Ministre des Affaires Etrangères. On écrivit également à la Croix-Rouge irlandaise.

La réponse de la CRI de Dublin fut accompagnée d'un document qui enflamma les émotions des conseillers: une résolution du syndicat des Médecins de la Manche votée lors de deux réunions, à Saint-Lô en mai et à Coutances en juillet, avant d'être expédiée à Dublin. Dès lors que la souveraineté était rendue à leur pays, les médecins de la Manche voulaient reprendre le plein contrôle administratif en matière des services de santé. Tout en remerciant leurs bienfaiteurs irlandais, et en espérant que ceux-ci «comprendront la juste prétention des médecins français à servir eux-mêmes leur pays, si éprouvé par la guerre», ils réclamaient donc «le retour immédiat de l'hôpital irlandais sous la gestion administrative et médicale françaises».

Mais ce qui enragea véritablement le maire et ses conseillers

L'hôpital des ruines

municipaux, ce fut moins le texte de ce document que le fait que deux des conseillers, le docteur Bourdon et le docteur Philippe, avaient participé à sa rédaction et qu'ils s'en étaient tûs lors de la réunion du Conseil du 5 août. Une réunion extraordinaire du Conseil eut lieu mardi 17 septembre, pendant laquelle le maire informa les conseillers de la réponse de Dublin et de la résolution du syndicat des Médecins. Lavalley reprocha leur silence aux deux conseillers médicaux, qui, à leur tour, se mirent à se justifier en expliquant les motifs de la résolution du Syndicat départmental. Ils prétendirent que les médecins irlandais n'avaient ni respecté l'accord, rédigé au mois de janvier précédent, sur le règlement des conditions d'admission de l'hôpital, ni signé la convention, datant du mois de novembre, sur la gestion de l'hôpital après le départ des Irlandais. Selon cette convention, la Croix-Rouge française prendrait contrôle de l'hôpital pour une période de trois mois, une fois les Irlandais partis. La direction de l'hôpital passerait par la suite à un organisme municipal, la Commission administrative de l'Hospice de la ville de Saint-Lô. Au terme d'un débat orageux, le Conseil du 17 septembre mandata le maire de se rendre à Dublin pour mettre toutes ces questions au clair.

Entretemps, une grande manifestation d'amitié envers l'hôpital irlandais fut organisée dans la ville l'après-midi du samedi 21 septembre. Entre quatre et cinq mille personnes prirent part à cet événement, représentant diverses organisations et associations municipales et départementales. Ils portaient des banderoles en faveur du maintien de l'hôpital, et protestaient contre la demande du syndicat médical de l'arrondissement réclamant le départ immédiat de leurs bienfaiteurs. Après plusieurs discours, un cortège se rendit jusqu'à l'hôpital pour offrir des fleurs au personnel; et plus de 2,000 signatures s'apposèrent sur un document demandant la prolongation du séjour des Irlandais dans la ville.

Georges Lavalley partit pour Dublin le lendemain; il en revint enchanté par l'accueil qu'il y avait reçu. En plus, le maire pouvait maintenant clarifier trois points importants. On lui avait expliqué les difficultés financières de la CRI; on avait néanmoins consenti à la demande de prolonger le séjour des Irlandais pour deux mois supplémentaires, ce qui établit désormais la date définitive de leur départ au 31 décembre 1946. Enfin, la CRI avait consenti à ce que l'hôpital passe aux mains des autorités municipales de Saint-Lô après un interrègne de trois mois, au cours duquel la gestion en serait assurée par la CRF.

Du moment que tout était maintenant au clair, la réaction du syndicat des Médecins à la manifestation du 21 septembre semble plutôt malencontreuse. Quelques jours plus tard, le syndicat publia un long communiqué de presse, citant les raisons juridiques, sociales, financières et techniques de leur attitude vis-à-vis de l'hôpital irlandais. Cette remise en public de la querelle provoqua la démission des deux conseillers médicaux, les docteurs Bourdon et Philippe, lors de la réunion du Conseil municipal le 2 octobre.

À mesure que les mois d'hiver approchaient, et que l'affaire de l'hôpital irlandais occupait moins de place dans les pages de la presse saint-loise, médecins et infirmières irlandais faisaient leurs valises et s'apprêtaient à rentrer chez eux. Comme convenu, la Croix-Rouge française veillait pendant cette période de transition au recrutement de personnel local pour les remplacer. À partir du mois de janvier 1947, la Commission administrative de l'Hospice de Saint-Lô prit en charge la direction de l'hôpital.

Il y eut des soirées d'adieux: l'une au début de décembre pour remercier les infirmières partant le 5 décembre, un banquet officiel à l'hôpital le 19 décembre, auquel assista le Colonel McKinney. Lavalley profita de l'occasion pour honorer l'ancien directeur du titre de citoyen d'honneur de la ville.

Par un brouillard matinal le 2 janvier 1947, la plupart des

L'hôpital des ruines

Irlandais quittèrent Saint-Lô. Une foule de quelques centaines de personnes se réunit à la gare et, alors que les trains disparaissaient de vue, les Saint-Lois faisaient adieu de la main aux infirmières irlandaises, dont les bras étaient chargés de fleurs.

Épilogue

Tout en gardant son nom d'hôpital irlandais, l'hôpital continuait à servir la ville de Saint-Lô jusqu'en juin 1956. Pour des baraques en bois hâtivement installées et provisoires, cette période était un peu trop longue. Elles commençaient à pourrir et présentaient un grand risque d'incendie.

Néanmoins, le nouvel hôpital municipal, dont les architectes avaient déjà été nommés en 1946, fut finalement prêt à recevoir ses malades le 10 mai 1956. Le Colonel McKinney assista aux cérémonies d'ouverture.

Ce nouveau Centre Hospitalier Mémorial France-États-Unis ne pouvait pas présenter un plus grand contraste avec l'hôpital irlandais, de par ses dimensions, son innovation architecturale, son matériel technique. Dédié aux soldats américains et aux autres victimes de la bataille de l'été 1944, le Mémorial mit au jour son premier bébé le 26 juin. Vers la même date s'effectua un autre rite de passage, quand l'hôpital irlandais en entier déménagea dans l'aile occidental du nouvel hôpital. Au cours de deux journées, 140 malades, lits, médicaments, linge et matériel domestique furent transportés et installés dans le nouveau local à l'autre bout de la ville. L'hôpital irlandais n'existait plus.

Les baraques désormais vides devenaient de plus en plus délabrées; on finit par les démolir pour permettre la construction d'un nouveau lycée. Une seule baraque survit, pourtant, témoin du centre médical des années d'après-guerre.

Et les membres du personnel de l'hôpital irlandais? Que sont-ils devenus?

L'année passée à Saint-Lô occasionna plusieurs mariages: le chirurgien Paddy Carey et l'une des infirmières, Breda

Healing amid the ruins

O'Rahelly; le responsable des bâtiments, George Stewart, et l'infirmière radiographe, Julia Murphy; la secrétaire, Clare Olden, et un militaire britannique en poste à Bayeux; l'autre chirurgien, Freddie McKee, et une Saint-Loise, Simone Lefèvre. De manière plus indirecte, une ambulancière de la Croix-Rouge française, Jacqueline de Gromard, rencontra son mari irlandais, Heber MacMahon, lors d'une visite à Dublin chez son amie, la docteur Sullivan, peu de temps après la rentrée de celle-ci.

Les membres du personnel rentrèrent en Irlande pour la plupart, pour poursuivre leur carrière dans divers hôpitaux ou ailleurs. Certains trouvèrent d'abord du travail en Grande Bretagne; d'autres, comme le docteur Leahy, y sont restés. Tommy Dunne, le magasinier qui remplaça Samuel Beckett, travailla pour la CRI à Dublin; le pharmacien, Timmy O'Driscoll, partit à Londres. Quant à l'aumônier, le père Brendan Hynds, il retrouva une paroisse au centre de l'Irlande. Parmi le personnel féminin, un certain nombre allaient retrouver diverses occupations.

Les amitiés persistaient parmi les membres du groupe, et l'on se réunissait de temps à autre pour boire un verre et chanter *Ma Normandie* ou *Nos Vieux Pommiers*.

La correspondance entre les Théot et quelques membres du personnel irlandais témoignent de l'attachement pour Saint-Lô vivement ressenti par ceux-ci. Certains y sont rentrés. Michael Killick, technicien du laboratoire d'analyses, s'y est rendu avec sa jeune épouse lors de leur lune de miel, invités des Théot. Le docteur Darley y retourna en 1947 pour rendre visite à ses amis normands. Bien des années plus tard, en 1995, l'infirmière Dilly Fahey est, elle aussi, retournée à Saint-Lô, où elle a rencontré par coïncidence une ancienne malade, Cécile Delannoë ainsi que Marie-Anne Théot. Toutes les trois ont chanté à cette occasion *Ma Normandie*, chanson que l'Irlandaise n'avait jamais oubliée. Elle allait mourir quelques mois plus tard, comme Cécile Delannoë moins de trois ans après.

Les Irlandais ne vécurent pas tous tant d'années. Arthur

L'hôpital des ruines

Darley mourut à Dublin à l'âge de quarante ans de tuberculose pulmonaire. La nouvelle de sa mort attrista Beckett et inspira un poème à son sujet, "Mort de A.D.". Jim Gaffney périt dans un accident d'avion au Pays de Galles en janvier 1952. En 1954, Marguerite Barrett mourut d'une leucémie, et Tim Boland d'un infarctus, comme d'ailleurs le chirurgien, Freddie McKee, six ans plus tard.

Destiné à devenir le plus connu des Irlandais de Saint-Lô, Samuel Beckett fut content, en janvier 1946, de quitter son poste à l'hôpital, qu'il trouvait épuisant. Effectivement il y avait joué simultanément, et avec beaucoup d'assiduité, plusieurs rôles: magasinier, interprète, ambulancier, professeur de français des infirmières. La CRI lui avait demandé de continuer de travailler pour leur compte à Paris, mais il refusa parce qu'il voulait se consacrer à plein temps à son écriture.

Et il écrivit. Les années suivantes furent des années extrêmement fertiles pour Beckett, aboutissant au succès sensationnel de la pièce *En attendant Godot*. C'est d'ailleurs à partir de son séjour normand que l'auteur allait écrire, pour la plupart du temps, en français.

Quant aux échos de Saint-Lô dans l'œuvre de cet auteur, on ne saurait dire avec certitude ce qui relève de son vécu dans la capitale des ruines. Tant de thèmes beckettiens — l'humour devant la misère et la souffrance, les allusions à la catastrophe et à la rédemption, pour n'en citer que quelques-uns — pourraient exprimer son expérience de la guerre en général, tout aussi bien que son génie artistique individuel. Sans nier d'autres sources littéraires ou philosophiques.

Son poème "Saint-Lô" (aujourd'hui taillé en pierre, en traduction française, au Centre Culturel de la ville) s'inspire sans doute de son époque saint-loise, mais il semble suggérer quelque chose de bien plus profond et plus large que la rivière (la Vire) qui marque son point de départ. Beckett a laissé d'autres écrits sur l'hôpital irlandais: notamment le texte écrit pour la radio irlandaise, *The Capital of the Ruins* [La Capitale des

Ruines], et un poème posthume, à l'esprit plus moqueur, "Antipepsis".

On pourrait dire finalement que la véritable découverte de Beckett à Saint-Lô fut une connaissance approfondie de ses compatriotes. Paradoxalement, il avait rencontré dans la ville normande un échantillon plus large d'Irlandais et d'Irlandaises que dans les milieux sociaux relativement restreints de son quartier natal de Dublin, Foxrock, et de Trinity College.

Conclusion

La mission normande de la Croix-Rouge irlandaise s'insère dans un contexte d'aide médicale à la France qui remonte jusqu'à la Guerre de 1870, pendant laquelle un corps d'ambulanciers irlandais fut présent dans le nord de la France sur plusieurs mois. La guerre finie, on les remercia vivement.

De même, au 20e siècle, une série de cérémonies officielles témoigne de la reconnaissance envers les bénévoles de l'hôpital irlandais. En avril 1948 ce fut la présentation des médailles de la Reconnaissance à la Légation française à Dublin; quinze ans plus tard, en mai 1971, lors du 25e anniversaire de l'inauguration de l'hôpital irlandais, ce fut un vin d'honneur et une autre remise de médailles à l'Ambassade de France à Dublin; plus récemment, le 7 avril 1996, une commémoration du cinquantenaire de l'inauguration s'est tenue à Saint-Lô; et enfin, le 27 octobre 1998, une délégation saint-loise est venue présenter à la Croix-Rouge de Dublin le livre d'or de l'hôpital, contenant plus de 500 témoignages et signatures d'anciens malades et de leurs proches. L'occasion était d'autant plus émouvante que le livre fut présenté par une personne redevable aux médecins irlandais de sa vie: Maurice Lerebourg, qui avait passé six mois de son enfance à se faire soigner par eux.

Et pourtant, malgré tant de cérémonies officielles, des vestiges de la honte et de la culpabilité ressenties envers les visiteurs persistent chez les gens de la ville. Par un phénomène curieux de l'histoire, certaines périodes s'impriment de façon indélébile

L'hôpital des ruines

sur les mentalités d'une communauté, et le début de la reconstruction de la ville de Saint-Lô semble bien avoir été une telle période. Les gens se rappellent vivement leur amitié et leur soutien envers le personnel irlandais, ainsi que leur colère manifestée à l'encontre des médecins saint-lois.

Quelles leçons cette chronique peut-elle nous apprendre? Un des traits saillants de l'histoire de l'hôpital irlandais c'est la lenteur de son évolution: de sa réalisation, d'abord, et ensuite de l'annonce du départ des Irlandais. Si la date du départ avait été clairement décidée et annoncée à l'avance, il est probable que les médecins de la Manche se seraient sentis moins frustrés et moins impatients. On aurait pu sans doute éviter une bonne part des malentendus qui se dégagent de l'affaire de l'hôpital irlandais. En même temps, il faut ajouter une autre conséquence du rythme ralenti de l'établissement de l'hôpital: les contacts sociaux entre citadins et Irlandais qui en découlèrent. Ce qui, à son tour, explique le ressentiment de la population envers les médecins, dont la communication semblait d'une impolitesse inadmissible, dirigée non seulement contre un groupe de médecins et d'infirmières étrangers, mais contre un groupe d'amis.

L'hôpital irlandais, vu les difficultés de communication et étant donné la politique confuse de la France de 1944–45, fut à plusieurs égards une réussite impressionnante. Dans le cadre de l'Irlande, la valeur de l'aide apportée à Saint-Lô représentait une somme importante. La CRI avait décidé de concentrer son aide en un seul endroit. De plus, les Irlandais, dont beaucoup venaient de milieux ruraux ou de petites villes comparables, pouvaient retrouver une certaine familiarité dans la ville de Saint-Lô, avec sa population d'après-guerre de cinq ou six mille habitants.

Il faut dire que ce qui comptait, finalement, c'est ce que l'hôpital irlandais représentait pour les citadins qu'il servait. Lors du vin d'honneur offert aux infirmières en décembre 1946, le maire, Georges Lavalley, leur rendit hommage en des termes vibrants: «Le geste magnifique de votre pays, ce geste de grande fraternité dans les ruines d'une petite ville de France, est une bien belle page écrite au livre d'or de son histoire et aussi un acte de foi dans l'avenir de Saint-Lô...». Le projet de la Croix-Rouge irlandaise — projet qui, pour les Irlandais, n'avait signifié qu'un devoir — symbolisait, pour les habitants de la capitale des ruines, quelque chose de bien plus important. Plus que l'aide médicale, il signifiait l'espoir dans l'avenir.

Irish Red Cross staff at the *hôpital irlandais*, Saint-Lô

Barrett, Marguerite (1889–1964) (Normandy) receptionist/interpreter and sewing-room supervisor: Oct. 1945–Apr. 1946

Beckett, Samuel B. (1906–89) (Foxrock, Co. Dublin) interpreter and storekeeper: Aug. 1945–Jan. 1946

Boland, Daniel Timothy (Tim) (*d.* 1954) (Co. Kildare) gynaecologist and obstetrician: Nov. 1945–Dec. 1946

Brennan, Julia Anne (Claremorris, Co. Mayo) nurse: Apr. 1946 onwards

Bridgeman, Joseph, driver/mechanic: May–Dec. 1946

Buckley, Angela (*d.* 1998) (Ballyhaunis, Co. Mayo) nurse (medicine): Jan.–Dec. 1946

Burke, Johanna (Joan) (Clonmel, Co. Tipperary) nurse: Jan.–Dec. 1946

Carey, Patrick (Paddy) (1920–93) (Dublin and London) surgeon: Apr.–Dec. 1946

Conroy, Kathleen, assistant matron and housekeeping sister: Nov. 1945–autumn 1946

Corrigan, Mary Agnes (Co. Roscommon) nurse: Apr.–Dec. 1946

Crowley, Mary Frances (Wexford) matron: Dec. 1945–autumn 1946

Cullinan, Mary Josephine (Mary Joe) (Co. Galway) nurse: summer–Dec. 1946

Cunningham, Nora (Ballyhaunis, Co. Mayo) charge nurse (medicine): Nov. 1945–Dec. 1946

Darley, Arthur Warren (1908–48) (Dublin) general physician (tuberculosis and outpatients units): Aug. 1945–Dec. 1946

Doherty, Ann (Dublin) nurse: Jan.–Dec. 1946

Doherty, Margaret ('Doc') (Abbeyfeale, Co. Limerick) theatre nurse: Nov. 1945–Dec. 1946

Dunne, Eileen A. (Portlaoise, Co. Offaly) nurse: Jan.–Dec. 1946

Dunne, Tommy (Dublin) storeman: Aug. 1945–Dec. 1946

Fahey, Bridget (*d.* 1996) (Dilly) (Ballindine, Co. Mayo) nurse: Jan.–Dec. 1946

Fitzgerald, Maurice E. J. (France) transport supervisor: Oct. 1945–spring 1946

Fitzpatrick, Mary (Madeleine) (Cavan) charge nurse (medicine): Nov. 1945–Dec. 1946

Gaffney, James Cyril (Jim) (1913–52) (Dublin) pathologist (and acting director: winter 1945/46), Aug. 1945–Aug. 1946

Gumbrielle, Edward Peter Paul (Ned) (1916–85) (Dublin) anaesthetist: Jan.–Dec. 1946

Healy, Teresa (Terry) (Lusk, Co. Dublin) nurse: Apr.–Dec. 1946

Hynds, Brendan (1908–93) (Co. Westmeath) chaplain: Jan.–Dec. 1946

Kelly, Brigid (Breda) (Co. Tyrone) nurse: Apr.–Dec. 1946

Killick, Michael Brendan (Dublin) laboratory technician: Aug. 1945–Dec. 1946

Leahy, Desmond John (Co. Clare and Bath) principal physician, director (from summer 1946): Sept. 1945–Dec. 1946

Leavy, Margaret (Nano) (Co. Meath) nurse: Apr.–Dec. 1946

MacDermott, Ita (Maeve) (*d.* 1998) (Dublin) maternity sister: Nov. 1945–Dec. 1946

McDermott, Angela (Newry, Co. Down) nurse (physiotherapist/masseuse): Mar.–Dec. 1946

McGee, Phyllis (Co. Louth) nurse: Apr.–Dec. 1946

McGriskin, Moira (Co. Leitrim) nurse: Jan.–Dec. 1946

McKee, Frederick Francis (Freddie) (1916–60) (Belfast) surgeon: Aug. 1945–July 1946

McKinney, Thomas Joseph (1887–1973) director: Aug. 1945–May 1946

McNicholas, Patrick J. (Paddy) (1919–90) (Co. Galway)

ophthalmologist: Jan.–Dec. 1946

Malone, Margaret (Dublin) theatre nurse: summer–Dec. 1946

Martin, Margaret Mary (Newry, Co. Down) charge nurse: Nov. 1945–Dec. 1946

Mullally, Eileen (Nellie) (Mullingar, Co. Westmeath) charge nurse: Nov. 1945–Dec. 1946

Murphy, Julia, nurse-radiographer: Nov. 1945–Dec. 1946

Murphy, Roderick, laboratory technician: May–Dec. 1946

O'Brien, Margaret, charge nurse: Nov. 1945–Dec. 1946

O'Connor, Nora (Liscannor, Co. Clare) nurse: summer–Dec. 1946

O'Doherty, Agnes C., shorthand typist: autumn 1945–Dec. 1946

O'Driscoll, Ellen (Ella) (Valentia, Co. Kerry) nurse: Apr.–Dec. 1946

O'Driscoll, Timothy J. (Timmy) (Co. Cork) chemist: Jan.–Dec. 1946

Olden, Clare (Cork) secretary: Oct. 1945–Dec. 1946

O'Mahony, Denis, function unclear: winter 1946

O'Rahelly, Breda (Co. Tipperary) theatre nurse: Jan.–Dec. 1946

O'Reilly, Anne M. ('Amor') (Co. Cavan) charge nurse (medicine): Nov. 1945–Dec. 1946

Ryan, Brendan (Dublin) accountant: Aug.–Dec. 1946

Shannon, Rose Monica (Mona) (Dublin) nurse: summer–Dec. 1946

Smith, Dorothy (Dorry) (1900–67) (Cavan) administrator: Nov. 1945–Dec. 1946

Stafford, George (Gorey) function unclear: winter 1946

Stewart, George, buildings supervisor: Oct. 1945–Dec. 1946

Sullivan, Catherine (Kitty) (*d.* 1972) (Howth, Dublin) physician (outpatients): late spring–Dec. 1946

Thompson, Alan H. (1906–74) (Co. Wexford) head of medicine: Aug.–Oct. 1945

Trehy, Margaret (Madge) (Tipperary) nurse: Jan.–Dec. 1946

Notes to the English text

The notes which follow give some sources and further details relating to the text. References may be followed up by consulting the sources and bibliography.

1: Saint-Lô, 1944, *capitale des ruines*
The principal sources used for this chapter include Boivin et al.; Lantier; Lefrançois; Patry; and *Témoignages des Saint-Lois de 44*.
page 1   *'sufficient for the total reconstruction of Saint-Lô.'* Beckett, 'The Capital of the Ruins', typescript, p. 3
page 4   *put up a tenacious resistance.* On the rights and wrongs of the Allies' strategy, see Gordon, pp. 193–8.
page 6   *187,000 lost their homes. Manche 1945*, pp. 10–11.
—   *half that figure lost their lives.* The precise number of fatal casualties in Saint-Lô is difficult to determine. Estimates range from 450 (Boivin et al., p. 25, n. 20) to 800 (Florentin, p. 12). A report, sent 29/1/45 by the Mayor of Saint-Lô to the Mayor of Perth, mentions 500 victims. (Archives of the Saint-Lô-Perth Committee, File PTC 517/9. A. K. Bell Library, Perth.) As corpses were still being found months later, the upper figure (of 800) is probably more accurate.
page 9   *sustained enormous casualties.* Lantier, *44 jours*, p. 134. On the casualties, including accidental ones, sustained by the Allied forces, see Gordon, p. 241, n. 36. German casualties—3,300 lost in nine days—were low in comparison (Gordon, p. 197; Florentin, p. 175).
page 10 *'as a monument to the havoc wrought by war'.* Patry, p. 56.
page 11 *the fate of Saint-Lô was hanging in the balance.* Lefrançois, p. 148. In some ways, of course, the local insecurity merely reflected a national sense of insecurity just after the war.
page 12 *restored to its rightful home as soon as possible. Ouest-France*, 11/6/45: 'Pour saluer le général de Gaulle la Normandie avait semé dans ses ruines des drapeaux, des fleurs et des "vivats!"'; and *'La visite du général de Gaulle dans la Manche'*, which carries a photograph of the French leader walking through the ruins of Saint-Lô.
page 13 *'It's pretty well disaster personified.'* Undated typescript describing Saint-Lô after the summer of 1944, by Jean Éparvier, entitled *'J'ai voulu revoir la Normandie . . . j'ai vu la misère et le dénuement'*. Archives of the Saint-Lô-Perth Committee, File PTC 517/9 (A. K. Bell Library, Perth). (Translated by the author.)

Notes to the English text

2: The Irish Red Cross hospital unit
The principal sources used for this chapter include McNamara; *Irish Red Cross Monthy Bulletin (IRC Bulletin)*; the Archives of the Irish Red Cross Society; Irish Military Archives, file 82804; Irish National Archives, D/FA 419/7 and D/Taoiseach File S13332; Archives of the Quai d'Orsay, files C60 1 and Z 219—3; RCSI Nursing Faculty Archive, Mary Crowley's papers.

page 15 *'the Irish bringing gifts'*. Beckett, 'The Capital of the Ruins', typescript, p. 2.

page 16 *which raised some £184,000.* IRC Secretary to Government Secretary, 26/9/45, National Archives, D/FA 419/7; 'The Irish Hospitals Sweeps' Charitable Achievements' brochure, no date, in Mary Crowley's papers, Archive of the Faculty of Nursing, RCSI. For a colourful account of the Irish Sweep, see Webb, who gives a higher figure for the wartime Red Cross sweeps intake, setting it at £218,360 (p. 138). Compared to the bonanzas of the thirties, wartime revenue from the sweeps was relatively low.

— *eight foolscap pages.* Irish Red Cross Archives, Miscellaneous Minute Book: Minutes of Ambulance Units and Relief Units Committee, 1943; Military Archives, 82804: 'General Plan for a Mobile Relief Unit' and 'Inventory of Equipment for Light Mobile Surgical Units'.

— *'join British Units as individuals'*. National Archives, D/Taoiseach File S13332, letter from Joseph Walshe to Department of the Taoiseach, 28/10/43.

page 17 *'supplies of medical and surgical equipment'*. McNamara, IRC secretary, to Mathieu, 24/8/44, Military Archives, 82804.

— *Ireland's envoy accredited to France.* See Keogh, pp. 182–91. A further account of the diplomatic background is provided by Gaffney, in a forthcoming article in *Études Irlandaises*, 24, 1, 1999.

page 18 *'France being the closest'*. Archives, Quai d'Orsay, File C 60 1, Laforcade to Paris, 19/9/44.

page 19 *'Ambulance Unit to France during the war of 1870'*. IRC *Bulletin*, 4, October 1944, p. 287. The *Bulletin* of 5 August 1945, pp. 234–5 gives the text of Maguire's speech in the Shelbourne hotel, on 29 June 1945. The Shelbourne speech again recalled the 1870 Ambulance Unit, which had consisted of over 100 men, ten horses and five carriages. Arriving in France in October 1870, it had served until the end of the Franco-Prussian war. For an account of the 1870 Unit, see the reminiscences of M. A. Leeson and Dr Richard Ryan; the *Irish Press*, 6/10/44; and the articles by J.

Fleetwood and G. Hayes-McCoy.

— *'and in some areas are practically non-existent.'* IRC Bulletin, 4, October 1944, p. 287.

page 20 *levels of pay being offered were reasonable.* Salaries ranged from £1,000 per annum for senior medical officers to £150 for male unmarried nurses and £100 for female nurses, exclusive of uniform allowance, subsistence and travelling expenses. (RCSI Nursing Faculty Archive, Mary Crowley's papers, 'Conditions of Service for Proposed Hospital to be set up in France'.) The IRC's intention to pay nurses' salaries at rates comparable to those at home is evident in a clause, laid down by a co-ordinating sub-committee meeting on 17 May 1945, specifying that the Saint-Lô rates would be 'subject to alterations in the scale of pay made by the Nursing Association.' (IRC Archives.) Moreover, conditions governing nurses' leave of absence were being worked out with the Department of Local Government. When in Saint-Lô, staff salaries could be paid direct into the individual's bank in Ireland, with a certain amount sent in francs for local use. Given the volatility and weakness of the French currency this was the safest option. (Communication, 27/3/98, from Dr Desmond Leahy.)

— *after years on the sidelines.* Some of the medical personnel had relatives who served in the British forces: Nurse Mary Corrigan, for example, had had a cousin killed on D-Day. (JCG, letter to his mother, 25/6/46: 'One of the nurses—Miss Corrigan from Roscommon—went to Bayeux the other day to take a picture of her cousin's grave there. Killed on D-Day (6/6/44) he lies with 5,000 others in a beautifully kept cemetery; she took her picture—a close-up of the grave of Gunner Mullen, R.A.; and another with the cathedral in the background.') Dorothy Smith's brother had served in the Great War and a cousin of Tim Boland's had worked as a surgeon during the 1940s in a field hospital in England.

page 21 *a long and frustrating wait before embarking for France.* Some of this frustration may have been the cue for a Dáil question, tabled 8/3/45, by Deputy James Larkin (Jr) to the Minister for External Affairs, asking for a definite date for the hospital's departure to France. (National Archives, D/Taoiseach, S13332).

— *'every department fully equipped and staffed'.* Mary Crowley, Soroptimist Club address, 23/11/48 (RCSI Nursing Faculty Archive, Mary Crowley's papers).

page 22 *'if not available.'* Mary Crowley, Soroptimist Club address, 23/11/48 (RCSI Nursing Faculty Archive, Mary Crowley's papers). A comprehensive 46 foolscap pages listing the supplies for Normandy

Notes to the English text

shows that no item, medical or domestic, was assumed to be available locally. (In a set of Miss Crowley's papers kindly lent by Miss Bridie Walsh.)

page 22 *'They were American planes.'* O'Regan and Dearey, p. 111.

page 23 *'ruined, isolated houses or villages, particularly at cross-roads, marked its path.'* IRC Bulletin, 5, June 1945, pp. 165–6.

page 24 *'Help —much help—will be needed.'* Ibid., p. 166.

— *these were approved by Michael Scott.* Scott's report on the French plans was read to the IRC's Co-ordinating Sub-Committee of the Continental Mobile Relief Unit Committee on 21/6/45 (IRC Archives: Miscellaneous Minute Book, 24/5/45–25/2/49).

page 24 *'consisting of personnel and equipment.'* Minutes of IRC Central Council meeting, 20/4/45 (IRC Archives). Exactly why the Paris authorities insisted on Ireland sending both staff and equipment is not clear.

page 25 *in Dublin in late May 1945.* IRC Archives: Minutes of the Co-ordinating Subcommittee of the Continental Mobile Relief Unit Committee, 31/5/45. His appointment was approved at an Executive Committee meeting, 8/6/45. (Beckett was paid £300—the same salary as the matron, presumably acknowledging his dual role as interpreter/storekeeper.)

— *farm labourer in return for food.* Knowlson, pp. 297–339; Cronin, pp. 309–40.

— *'if possible, a fluent French speaker'.* Minutes of the IRC Co-ordinating Subcommittee of the Continental Mobile Relief Unit Committee meeting, 2/5/45.

page 26 *to be microfilmed for British intelligence.* On Beckett's Resistance work, see Knowlson, pp. 303–15.

— *'food requirements of the Unit for six months, are being taken.'* IRC Bulletin, 5, August 1945, p. 230. When in Saint-Lô, the hospital complemented its supplies of tinned and dried foods with fresh local fruit, vegetables, cheeses and seafoods. Unlike Paris, Normandy did not suffer from postwar food shortages, despite some rationing. Jim Gafffney comments to his sister, Maureen, 31/8/45: 'We will not lose weight here.'

3: A hospital of wooden huts

The principal sources used for this chapter include the letters to his family from the late James Gaffney (JCG); two letters to MacGreevy from Beckett; and various conversations with former staff members or their relatives.

page 28 *'But I think that to the end of its hospital days it will be called*

[151]

Healing amid the ruins

the Irish Hospital.' Beckett, 'The Capital of the Ruins', typescript, p. 3.

— *'No lodging of course of any kind.'* Beckett, letter to Thomas MacGreevy, 19/8/45 (TCD Library, Manuscripts Room).

— *an active member of the French Red Cross.* Beckett, letter to Thomas MacGreevy, 19/8/45 (TCD Library, Manuscripts Room); cf. P. Gaffney, *'Just* a quibble: a note on Beckett's handwriting', *French Studies Bulletin,* Winter 1997, pp. 16–17; letter to the author from Denis de Kergorlay, 17/6/97.

— *'a tune of which I am tired.'* Beckett, letter to Thomas MacGreevy, 19/8/45 (TCD Library, Manuscripts Room). Beckett writes of more important concerns in the same letter, such as the death of friends who had been deported during the war. These tragedies probably left him less sympathetic towards his countrymen's exasperation over the delays.

page 29 *'so the language is no trouble.'* JCG, letter to his mother, 31/8/45.

— *'boarded up cellars, on mattresses.'* JCG, letter to his sister Maureen, 31/8/45.

page 30 *'the others are being wired or otherwise finished'* JCG, letter to his sister Maureen, 31/8/45.

— *'superintended also by French guards with rifles.'* JCG, letter to his sister Maureen, 31/8/45.

page 31 *'also lots of thread (for the ladies, we presume)'.* JCG, letter to his sister Maureen, 31/8/45.

— *had somehow to be be filled in France.* JCG, letters to his sister Nora, 2/10/45; his sister Josie, 4/10/45; his father, 16/10/45; and his brother-in-law, Christy Haugh, 28/10/45.

— *'to see and hear running water again.'* JCG, letter to his brother Maurice, 10/9/45.

— *'some dodge all the time'.* JCG, letter to his sister Maureen, 20/9/45.

page 32 *'brush our clothes, etc.'* JCG, letter to his mother, 9/10/45.

— *'iron paths around the hospital'.* JCG, letter to his sister Nora, 22/10/45.

— *crates which had carried supplies from Ireland.* JCG, letter to his sister Josie, 4/10/45.

— *'began to remove it, God knows where.'* JCG, letter to his sister Maureen, 31/8/45.

page 33 *a piano from a US base at Carentan.* Maurice Fitzgerald and George Stewart were involved in a crash in late spring 1946, when driving one of the hospital's ambulances. A French lorry carrying mine disposal experts collided with them, and they both suffered

Notes to the English text

facial injuries, Stewart more seriously than Fitzgerald. After this crash, Maurice's wife joined her husband in Saint-Lô for a while. (Conversation with Mrs Meave Fitzgerald, 7 /2/98.)

page 34 *'knocking the head off with a spanner.'* Communication from Dr Desmond Leahy, 27/3/98.

— *'penicillin could not effect a cure of that condition.'* Communication from Dr Desmond Leahy, 15/4/98.

— *'in Dublin its price is about 15s.'* JCG, letter to his brother Maurice, 3/10/45. Penicillin in 1946 came in powder form; it was mixed with sterile water and given by means of injection. (Telephone conversation with Dr Desmond Leahy, 30/9/98). In the spring of 1945, the IRC had ordered 20,000,000 units of penicillin from Fannin's medical suppliers in Dublin (Minutes of the Co-ordinating Sub-Committee of the Continental Mobile Relief Unit meeting, 11/5/45); in February 1946, they were ordering a further supply, as it was felt 'desirable to keep four or five million units of penicillin in the Hospital' (Minutes of the French Hospital Unit Committee meeting, 20/2/46). This probably represents an amount surplus to the hospital's own immediate requirements, as the society aimed to be (in Colonel McKinney's words) 'more than self-contained in the matter of medical supplies to permit of a distribution of our surplus in the not improbable event of our receiving a request to this effect.' (*IRC Bulletin*, June 1945, 5, p. 164.)

— *as a precaution against theft.* Conversation, February 1998, with Mrs Meave Fitzgerald and Mrs Blánaid O'Rahilly. A letter of Jim Gaffney's describes how, on returning to Saint-Lô from a period of leave in Ireland, his suitcase, which contained some cocaine, literally fell out of an open truck on the way from Paris. Probably because of its contents, the luggage was never recovered, although the police had been notified. (Letter to his mother, 3/3/46).

page 35 *'the French Red Cross, for reasons not clear, insist on an Irish staff.'* Beckett, letter to Thomas MacGreevy, 19/8/45 (TCD Library, Manuscripts Room).

— *'they will need the services of a pathologist at any rate.'* JCG, letter to his sister Maureen, 31/8/45.

— *'we modified our plan of operations'.* JCG, letter to his brother Maurice, 10/9/45.

— *'some of which only gets to our ken.'* JCG, letter to his brother Maurice, 3/10/45.

page 36 *a local doctor's certificate before being admitted.* The terms of these guidelines were read out to the town council at a meeting in February 1946; they were also summarised by Dr Bourdon at the

Healing amid the ruins

meeting of 17/9/46. (*Archives municipales*, Saint-Lô: Minutes of the *Conseil municipal*, 11/2/46 and 17/9/46.)

page 37 *'went so far as to refer to it as* "magnifique"*!* JCG, letter to his brother-in-law Christy Haugh, 28/10/45.

— *transferred from demolished houses in Paris.* 'Touching Tributes of War-Stricken People', *Irish Independent*, 15/4/46.

— *slept by the roadside.* Knowlson, pp. 349–50.

— *a French Red Cross driver who was to bring them home.* Communication from Dr Desmond Leahy, 15/4/98. Leahy remarked that such a walk would not have been difficult for Beckett, who had been accustomed to long walks in the Dublin hills.

— *double doors fitted by the hospital's carpenter.* Communication from Dr Desmond Leahy, 15/4/98.

page 38 *'all received the hospitality of the house'.* Mary Crowley, Soroptimist address, 23/11/48. (RCSI Nursing Faculty Archive.)

— *'the Irish equivalent of calvados.'* Lelièvre, *Terre Normande*, March/April 1946, p. 14. (Translation by the author.)

— *'it's time-consuming and so we will share the job.'* JCG, letter to his brother-in-law Christy Haugh, 28/10/45.

— *'black cloth and Latin testaments for the clergy'.* *Perthshire Advertiser*, 13/10/45, p. 7: 'Perth Party's Visit to Saint-Lô'.

page 39 *had died of a stroke before he arrived home.* JCG, letter to his mother, 18/12/45; Beckett, letter to Thomas MacGreevy, 21/12/45 (TCD Library, Manuscripts Room).

— *'the work I know most about.'* JCG, letter to his mother, 18/12/45.

— *'landmines and wartime conditions'.* Handwritten recollection signed by Mary Crowley (in a set of her papers kindly lent by Bridie Walsh); cf. Beckett's letter to Thomas MacGreevy, 21/12/45 (TCD Library, Manuscripts Room).

page 40 *was critically short of priests.* Information on Father Hynds was kindly supplied by Father Frank Kelly, Granard, Co. Longford, with whom Father Hynds worked for many years in later life. (Telephone conversation, 3/3/98). Cf. *Irish Press* cutting, late January 1946, in Military Archives, File G2/X/1369.

— *'somewhere between 45–55 patients.'* JCG, letter to his brother-in-law, Christy Haugh, 25/1/46.

— *fresh flowers adorning the wards and staff dining-room.* IRC Bulletin, 6, 1946, pp. 10–11. This is a reprint of the journalist's article carried by *La Manche Libre*, in its Saint-Lô edition, 2/12/45.

— *'I anyway am very glad to be going.'* Beckett, letter to Thomas MacGreevy, written from the Hôtel des Arcades, Dieppe, and dated

Notes to the English text

21/12/45 (TCD Library, Manuscripts Room).

page 41 *'as their bottlewasher in Paris.'* Ibid.

— *to bring it to Saint-Lô in January 1946.* O'Brien, *Journal of the Irish College of Physicians and Surgeons*, 19, 1990, p. 144; Cronin, p. 354. McMillan, p. 71, reports that Beckett later spoke of finding this rat poison as his last personal act of war.

— *'in every way a most likeable chap.'* JCG, letter to his sister Nora, 2/10/45.

— *'It was very thoughtful of him.'* JCG, letter to his sister Nora, 2/10/45.

page 42 *and under a good deal of stress.* Sometimes there would be a queue of 500 people waiting to see them. Madame Marie-Anne Théot remembers Drs Darley and Sullivan as being very overworked, under so much pressure that they would often refuse their cup of tea, offering it to a patient instead. (Conversation, Saint-Lô, 24/3/1998.)

4: No ramshackle affair

The principal sources used for this chapter include the letters to his family of JCG; communications from Dr Desmond Leahy; conversations with Meave Fitzgerald, the late Angela Buckley and former patients; and relevant papers in the *Archives départementales de la Manche*.

page 43 *'the best that priority can command.'* Beckett, 'The Capital of the Ruins', typescript, p. 1.

— *on 7 April 1946.* Accounts of the day, giving texts of the official speeches, are found in various press reports in France and Ireland, including *Irish Press*, 8/4/46 and 15/4/46; *Irish Independent*, 15/4/46; *France Croix-Rouge*, 2, June 1946; and *Ouest-France*, 8/4/46.

— *December of the previous year.* One of Jim Gaffney's tasks, as the hospital's acting director during Colonel McKinney's compassionate leave after his wife's death, was to start organising the official opening, which was to be 'a very big affair'. (JCG, letter to his mother, 18/12/45.)

page 45 *'with a smaller dance here in our recreation hut, about 3 a.m.'* JCG, letter to his sister Maureen, 12/4/46.

— *'laid out on top of or under the tables.'* Letter to the author from Mrs Isabelle McNicholas, 22/7/98.

— *and an administrative staff of nine.* In addition to the IRC staff, the French Red Cross supplied ambulance drivers, a concierge and some kitchen and laundry staff. A retired hospital administrator was employed on the admissions desk. About ten French nationals, as well as about thirteen German POWs, one Italian and some Poles formed this ancillary staff, recruited locally. *France Croix-Rouge,* June 1946, p. 3; Dr Desmond Leahy, 31/9/98; Mary Crowley, Soroptomist Club Address, 23/11/48.

page 46 *'standards of the Dublin hospitals are among the highest.'* IRC Bulletin, 6, June 1946, 'And the Cause of it All', pp. 148–9. Written by a Red Cross delegate who had attended the official opening, this account is signed 'J.P.S.', initials which stand quite probably for Dr J.P. Shanley, a member of the IRC Central Committee.

— *no record that the piece was ever broadcast.* Besides the original in RTE's Archives, a copy of the typescript, 'The Capital of the Ruins', is included in Mary Crowley's papers, RCSI Nursing Faculty Archive. It has been published by Eoin O'Brien in *The Beckett Country,* pp. 333–7, and in his article, 1990; and by Dougald McMillan, in the Festschrift for Beckett's 80th birthday, *As No Other Dare Fail*, pp. 73–6. It also appears in Gontarski, pp. 275–8. On the confusion surrounding the broadcast, see Gontarski, pp. 285–6. The present author will give a more detailed account in a forthcoming issue of the *Irish University Review* (29, 2, autumn/winter 1999).

page 47 *'cette cité blanche, aux salles claires et fleuries'.* Lelièvre, *Terre Normande,* 3, March/April 1946, p. 14.

— *and its meticulous cleanliness.* Desile, 'L'histoire de l'hôpital irlandais (suite)', *Manche Libre,* 17/12/78.

— *'a good German chemist'.* JCG, letter to his mother, and postcard to his brother-in-law Christy Haugh, 18/12/45.

page 48 *'no disaster could shake.'* Kees van Hoek, *Sunday Express,* 7 July 1946.

— *'for the patient he had brought.'* Marie-Anne Théot, memoir written in 1997, translated into English by Jacqueline Fontanel.

page 49 *'It was the least we could do.'* Marie-Anne Théot, memoir, 1997. Comparing the Irish doctors' professionalism to a kind of religious vocation (*sacerdoce),* she recalls an occasion when Dr Tim Boland, the gynaecologist/obstetrician, left a slice of her cherry tart unfinished on his plate, to deal with an urgent call.

— *involved in this reconstruction process in Saint-Lô.* Desramé, pp. 35–6.

— *'Normandy's "Irishtown" appears positively luxurious.'* Kees Van Hoek, *Sunday Express,* 7/7/46.

page 50 *as Beckett reported in June 1946.* Beckett, 'The Capital of the Ruins', typescript, p. 2.

— *while playing in a meadow.* JCG, letter to his sister Nora, 22/

Notes to the English text

10/45.

— *a child who had drunk boiling liquid.* O'Brien, 'Samuel Beckett at Saint-Lô—"Humanity in Ruins"', *Journal of the Irish Colleges of Physicians and Surgeons*, 19, 1990, p. 141.

— *skin grafts along his left arm and abdomen.* Interview with former patients, organised by the Shanaghy Association, Musée du Bois-Jugan, Saint-Lô, 17/5/97; cf. *Manche Libre*, 17/5/97: 'Souvenirs de l'hôpital irlandais: témoignage de Maurice Lerebourg'.

— *who was also asked to be the child's godfather.* Conversation with Dr Desmond Leahy, 2/9/98.

page 51 *'roses, rhododendrons, lilies, sweet pea, etc.'* JCG, letter to his mother, 17/7/46.

page 52 *the one song they all knew in Latin, the* Adeste Fideles. Madame Lemeray: *'On ne se comprenait pas du tout. Pas un mot.'* Interview organised by the Shanaghy Association, Musée du Bois-Jugan, Saint-Lô, 17/5/97.

— *that the staff's expenses should be reimbursed.* JCG, letter to his brother Maurice, 10/9/45.

— *dinner guests in the family home of the hospital architect, Monsieur Lafont.* JCG, *passim*; and letter to his sister Nora, 2/10/45.

— *a regular destination for weekends off duty.* The Archives départementales de la Manche (Cabinet du Préfet, File 1004 W 1727, R2) contain some correspondence between the Kergorlay family, the Irish Hospital and the *préfecture* about the villa. The property had two storeys over a basement, plus an attic storey as well as an outbuilding with more rooms. The lease, dated 30 April 1946, is for three years' duration, from 10 May 1946, with a provision that either party may rescind with three months' notice; and the contract stipulated a nominal annual rent of 25,000 francs payable by the IRC. Besides its use as a retreat for weary staff, it was to be used as a convalescent home for the hospital.

— *'the water is lukewarm all the time.'* JCG, letter to his father, 3/6/46.

page 53 *youth overflowing with zest for life.* Communication from Madame Brigitte de Kergorlay, 4/8/97.

— *'they hadn't thought that convents were such nice places.'* JCG, letter to his sister Maureen, 20/9/45.

— *'and an invitation to come and stay the night any time.'* JCG, letter to his sister Josie, 4/10/45.

page 54 *'trying "like hell"'to get to Ireland.'* JCG, letter to his sister Nora, 2/10/45.

— *'The Club is beside the British Embassy.'* JCG, letter to his

[157]

sister Maureen, 14/6/46.
— *"my parents come from County Clare".'* JCG, letter to his brother-in-law, Christy Haugh (who was also a Clare man), 25/1/46.

page 55 *'Irish songs which interested our visitors very much.'* JCG, letter to his sister Nora, 1/1/46.
— *being abroad for the first time in their lives.* Some pages in the album of Maeve MacDermott, for example, suggest an atmosphere of riotous fun in the nurses' quarters. (Album kindly shown to the author by Maeve MacDermott's nephew, Dermot MacDermott.) Staff sleeping-quarters, consisting of cubicles with partition walls not quite reaching the ceiling, doubtless helped to promote a convivial ambience.
— *evenings whiled away in a local brothel.* Knowlson, pp. 348–9.
— *'intemperance among the ruins'.* Beckett, letter to Thomas MacGreevy, 21/12/45 (TCD Library, Manuscripts Room).
— *invited to weddings and attended funerals.* Col. T. Mac Cionnaotha, 'Cumann Cros Dearg na hÉireann 'sa bhFrainnc', re-printed from *An Cosantóir, IRC Bulletin*, 6, 1946, pp.189–91 (p. 191).
— *the nurses were always singing.* Many former patients when interviewed conveyed this impression. (Interview with former patients, organised by the Shanaghy Association, Saint-Lô, 17/5/97.)

page 56 *'another on Christmas Eve afternoon for those under three.'* JCG, letter to his mother, 18/12/45. Cotton wool for Santa Claus's beard at one of these parties was supplied by the hospital's pathology laboratory (JCG, letter to his sister Nora, 1/1/46).
— *came to play in the hospital grounds.* Interview with former patients, organised by the Shanaghy Association, Saint-Lô, 17/5/97.
— *became a regular feature.* Conversation, 31/8/98, with Dr Desmond Leahy.
— *could readily relate.* Commenting on its size, Jim Gaffney refused to share the Parisian perspective of Saint-Lô: 'A small centre of population, the Parisian workmen here think it very provincial, think the people dull and depressed. We foreigners don't find them so.' (Letter to his brother Maurice, 3/10/45.)

5: The *affaire de l'hôpital irlandais*
The principal sources used for this chapter include IRC Archives; Irish Military Archives; Irish National Archives; O'Regan and Dearey. French sources include the *Archives départementales de la Manche*

Notes to the English text

the Minutes of Saint-Lô's *Conseil municipal*, 5/8/46, 17/9/46, 27/9/46, 2/10/46, 9/12/46 (*Archives municipales*, Saint-Lô); the following articles from *Manche-Libre*: 11/8/46: '*Le Départ de l'Hôpital Irlandais*', 22/9/46: '*Orage au Conseil Municipal: Monsieur Sainthuille, 2ème adjoint, M.M. Gablin et Leclerc démissionnent*', 6/10/46: '*L'Hôpital Irlandais restera à Saint-Lô jusqu'au 31 décembre*' and '*Saint-Lô-Hebdo—Les Docteurs Bourdon et Philippe donnent leur démission de Conseillers Municipaux*', 22/12/46: '*Saint-Lô-Hebdo—Le Colonel McKinney est venu à Saint-Lô comme représentant du Président de la Croix-Rouge Irlandaise. Il est fait citoyen d'honneur de notre ville*'; and from *Ouest-France*, Saint-Lô edition: 8/8/46: '*Au Conseil Municipal (suite): À l'unanimité, le Conseil décide d'intervenir auprès du Ministre d'Irlande en France afin de faire différer le départ de l'hôpital irlandais*', 19/9/46: '*La réunion extraordinaire et très orageuse du Conseil Municipal amène MM. Sainthuille, Leclerc et Gablin à se déclarer démissionnaires*', 26/9/46: '*L'affaire de l'hôpital irlandais: un communiqué du Syndicat départemental des Médecins de la Manche*', 30/9/46: '*La Mission Irlandaise restera à Saint-Lô jusqu'au 31 décembre 1946*', 1/10/46: '*Affaire de l'hôpital irlandais: Le conseil municipal se réunira mercredi pour entendre les explications des docteurs Bourdon et Philippe et prendre une décision définitive*', 5-6/10/46: '*L'Affaire de l'hôpital irlandais au Conseil Municipal: l'Assemblée n'a voté ni la confiance ni le blâme, ainsi que le demandaient les docteurs Bourdon et Philippe*', 7/10/46: '*L'affaire de l'hôpital irlandais—Le docteur Cuche se serait entretenu avec M. Lavalley de l'ordre du jour du syndicat des médecins*', 9/10/46: '*L'affaire de l'hôpital irlandais—Les docteurs Bourdon et Philippe réclament un vote du Conseil Municipal*', 11/10/46: '*L'affaire de l'hôpital irlandais—Un communiqué du syndicat départemental des médecins et une lettre de M. le Maire de Saint-Lô*', 13/10/46: '*Saint-Lô-Hebdo—'Pour mieux préciser!*', 22/10/46: '*Le dernier acte de l'affaire de l'hôpital irlandais—les docteurs Bourdon et Philippe ont donné officiellement leur démission de conseillers municipaux*'. Albert Desile, '*L'histoire de l'hôpital irlandais (suite)*', *Manche-Libre*, 17/12/78, provides a useful summary.

page 57 '*Whose exceptionally pia/ Mater hatched this grand idea/ Is not known.*' Samuel Beckett, 'Antipepsis', lines 9–11.

page 58 *the local doctors are rarely as excited*. Communication from Stephen O'Malley, 13/4/99, in relation to conflict between MSF and local surgeons in a hospital in Sierra Leone in 1997–8.

— '*About two years*'. *IRC Bulletin*, 6, 1946, p. 10.

— '*next March or April, hardly longer*.' JCG, letter to his mother,

17/7/46.
—   'on October 31st, next.' JCG, letter to his sister Nora, 3/8/46.
page 59 *'other war torn areas'*. Mary Crowley papers, Soroptimist paper, 23/11/48. (RCSI Nursing Faculty Archive.)
—   *having a meeting with the Polish Ministers for Agriculture and Health.* O'Regan and Dearey, pp. 112–17.
—   'a site to be found.' JCG, letter to his brother Maurice, 21/6/46.
—   'if it's really coming off.' JCG, letter to his sister Josie, 25/7/46.
page 60 'we are expecting some soon.' JCG, letter to his father, 22/8/46.
—   'as is the case at Saint-Lô.' Cutting from *Irish Press*, 22/6/46, in National Archives, D/Taoiseach, File S13332.
—   'they don't seem to be well-organised'. O'Regan and Dearey, p. 115.
—   'we didn't recognise them either, so it was impossible.' *Ibid*, p. 117.
page 61 'the Polish authorities are not hostile to the Catholic Church.' National Archives, D/FA, File 419/17, Extract from Minute of 28/1/1947.
—   'find a factory much more welcome!' National Archives, D/FA, File 419/1/14, Leathán mionuairisce, 16/1/47.
—   *£1,100 to £2,000 per month. Irish Press* cutting, 5/12/45, in Military Archives, File G2/X/1369; *IRC Bulletin*, 4, October 1944, pp. 287–8. The full cost of the hospital to the IRC Society was estimated in the order of £80,000, according to the Chairman's Report to Central Council, 21/3/47, p. 5. (IRC Archives: Central Council Minutes, vol. 3.)
—   'arises from lack of funds.' *IRC Bulletin*, 6, April 1946, p. 123.
page 62 *high infant and maternal mortality rates.* See Deeny, pp. 73, and 124–136, especially p. 127; and Barrington, pp. 161–2 and *passim*. In this connection, at least one dissenting voice had been raised, questioning the French hospital project; it was however silenced through censorship. File G2/X/1369, Irish Military Archives, preserves a censored letter to the *Evening Mail* signed 'Nurse', and dated 3/5/45: 'What about setting up a few hospitals in Dublin, or perhaps the people in Éire don't count? A number of sites are wanted badly in Dublin and County Dublin to build hospitals. When these hospitals have been built and set up, charity can go abroad.' The notion that charity should begin at home was conceivably shared by a section of Irish public opinion at the time.
—   'during the continuance of the present European War'. National Archives, D/Taoiseach, File S11071, ref. 2/96002.
—   *powers to raise funds through sweepstakes was unsuccessful.* A

legal opinion on behalf of the IRC argued that the term 'hospital', under Section 1 of the Public Hospitals Act 1933, could apply to medical treatment provided to patients outside the Irish Free State, since the Act did not specify where the treatment was to be carried out. It merely required that the institution affording the treatment be in Saorstát Éireann. Hence, it was argued that the IRC, one of the primary objects of which was to mitigate suffering throughout the world, could be deemed to be a hospital, with powers 'to manage and control a Sweepstake to raise money for the Hospitals Trust Fund.' However, the Attorney General rejected the argument. (National Archives, D/FA 419/7: letter from Mr McNamara, Irish Red Cross, to the Government Secretary; memorandum, D/Justice Ref. 88/45; letter from P. Ó Cinnéide, Assistant Secretary to the Government, to the Department of Justice, 5/1/46.)

page 63 *an extensive report on all of the hospital's departments.* IRC Chairman's Report to Central Council, 15/11/46, p. 4. (IRC Archives.)

page 64 *a visit there cost nothing.* Marcel Menant, interview organised by the Shanaghy Association, 17/5/97.

— *as they did everyone who asked them.* Lelièvre, *Terre Normande*, March/April 1946, p.14.

page 65 *to transfer ownership of the hospital to the town rather than the French Red Cross.* Drafted on 7 November 1945 and sent to the Manche *préfecture* the following month, the text of the agreement is found in a letter from Georges Lavalley to the *Préfet de la Manche*, 20/9/46 (*Archives départementales, Cabinet du Préfet*, File 1004 W 1727, R2). It was also presented by Dr Bourdon to the town council meeting of 17/9/46. Local anxieties about control of the hospital had already surfaced even before the Irish arrived in the town. In July 1945, Dr Bourdon's report to the town council on postwar hospital provision in Saint-Lô had expressed the view that the town was well able to run its own hospitals, without the involvement of the French Red Cross: 'Nous estimons que la Ville de Saint-Lô n'est pas une mineure, que la Commission Administrative de l'Hôpital est habilitée à gérer cet hôpital comme le sien propre.' (*Archives municipales,* Saint-Lô: Minutes of the *Conseil municipal,* 12/7/45.)

— *during a recent visit to the town.* Lavalley took this suggestion seriously enough to write to the Prefect of the Manche region, on 20 September. General Sicé, as the new President of the French Red Cross, had visited the *mairie* of Saint-Lô on 7 September 1946 and had apparently made it clear, to the consternation of those present, that he was not at all in favour of the November 1945 agreement. In his view, '*M. le Ministre de la Santé avait pris une décision qu'il ne lui appartenait pas de prendre, que l'Hôpital Irlandais, tout au moins en ce qui concerne le matériel, était, et resterait, la propriété de la Croix-Rouge Française, mais que cet organisme le laisserait à la disposition de la ville de Saint-Lô tout le temps nécessaire, mais un jour il lui serait enlevé.*' Faced with such a threat of dispossession, which went against all official declarations prior to this, Lavalley pleaded with the Prefect to intervene with the Ministry of Health, in order to ensure the adherence of all parties to the November agreement. (*Archives départementales, Cabinet du Préfet*, File 1004 W 1727, R2: Lavalley to *Préfet*, 20/9/46.)

page 66 *Nearly five thousand people marched in the protest.* Estimates of the size of the demonstration vary from 5,000 to 6,000 people: see *Ouest-France*, 23/9/46: '*Plus de 5,000 personnes manifestent en signe de protestation contre l'éventuel départ de la Mission Irlandaise*'; *Manche Libre*, 29/9/46: '*Saint-Lô Hebdo—six mille personnes manifestent pour que demeure à Saint-Lô le Corps Médical Irlandais*', with accompanying photograph; Albert Desile, '*L'histoire de l'hôpital irlandais (suite)*', *Manche-Libre*, 17/12/78. Official police reports are more conservative, all speaking of a crowd of 4,000 demonstrators: *Préfet (Manche)* to *Ministre de l'Intérieur*, 25/9/46: '*Manifestation à Saint-Lô en faveur du maintien de l'Hôpital Irlandais*'; *Préfet (Manche)* to *Direction Générale de la Sureté Nationale*, 23/9/46: '*Manifestation de la population Saint-Loise en faveur de l'Hôpital Irlandais*'; *Sous-Préfet de Coutances* to *Préfet (Manche)*, 23/9/46: '*Manifestation d'amitié envers l'Hôpital Irlandais*'; *Commissariat de Police de Saint-Lô* to M. le *Directeur Départemental des Services de Police*, Cherbourg, 22/9/46: '*Manifestation d'amitié envers l'Hôpital Irlandais de Saint-Lô, et de protestations contre la demande du syndicat des docteurs de l'arrondissement, demandant son départ*". All of these reports concur in describing a well behaved crowd, apart from one or two unruly elements who had shouted insults and threats as they marched past the homes of Dr Bourdon and Dr Philippe. (*Archives Départementales, Cabinet du Préfet*, File 1004 W 1727.)

page 67 '*l'affection que ces gens-là ont pour nous.*' *Ouest-France*, 30/9/46 (p. 3): '*La Mission irlandaise restera à Saint-Lô jusqu'au 31 décembre 1946*'.

page 68 '*very reasonable attitude*'. Beckett, letter to Thomas MacGreevy, 19/8/45 (TCD Library, Manuscripts Room).

— *during this interim period.* Archives of the Mémorial Hospital, Saint-Lô: correspondence, October-December 1946, between the Irish hospital and the council. See also IRC Chairman's Report to

Notes to the English text

Central Council, 15/11/46, p. 5 (IRC Archives).

— *A French matron was appointed by the middle of November.* Minutes of IRC Central Council meeting, 15/11/46. (IRC Archives.)

page 69 '*un acte de foi dans l'avenir de Saint-Lô*'. *Manche Libre*, 8/12/46. '*Saint-Lô-Hebdo—La Municipalité témoigne sa sympathie aux Irlandais à l'occasion du départ de onze infirmières.*' Ibid.

— '*l'Irlande sera toujours à l'honneur.*' Ibid.

page 70 '*embraced them and, in many cases, wept.*' Chairman's Report to IRC Central Council, 21/3/47, p. 5. (IRC Archives.) A handful of Irish staff stayed on until the end of the month, to tidy up the paper work and pay outstanding bills. These included Clare Olden, Agnes O'Doherty, Brendan Ryan (an accountant seconded from the *Irish Press* for the latter months of 1946) and the hospital's Director, Dr Desmond Leahy. (Communication from Dr Desmond Leahy, 26/6/98.)

6: As good as they gave

page 71 '*and their names forgotten*'. Beckett, 'The Capital of the Ruins', typescript, p. 3.

— '*in this universe become provisional*'. Ibid.

page 72 *and the nature of the electrical installations.* Manche-Libre, 2/11/52: '*Dans deux ans la population de Saint-Lô et ses environs sera privé d'hôpital*'; see also *Manche Libre*, 8/3/53: '*Des nouvelles de l'hôpital de Saint-Lô*'.

— *often haunted by the idea of the hospital catching fire.* Albert Desile, *Manche Libre*, 17/12/78: ' *L'histoire de l'hôpital irlandais (suite)*'.

— *together with the American ambassador to France, Douglas Dillon.* Manche-Libre, 13/5/56: '*Jour France-Amérique: Les deux nations inaugurent l'hôpital le plus moderne du monde construit par elles sur la terre meurtrie*'. The article features a photograph of Colonel McKinney receiving his *diplôme de Citoyen d'Honneur de la Ville de Saint-Lô*, apparently his second time receiving that honour. He was also decorated with the *Croix de chevalier de la Légion d'honneur*.

— *a shuttle service of trucks and vans borrowed for the occasion.* Manche-Libre, 1/7/56: '*En quelques heures, 140 malades ont quitté leurs baraquements de bois pour s'installer dans l'un des hôpitaux les plus modernes du monde*'; *Ouest-France*, 2/7/56: '*Le transfert de l'hôpital irlandais est terminé*'.

— *which was in use as late as the 1980s.* Communication, Bernadette Camon, Saint-Lô, May 1997.

page 73 *resumed their careers in different hospitals.* Information on different staff members was kindly provided by various sources, including Dr Nessa Carroll, Mrs Treasa McLoughlin, Mrs Simone McKee, Dr Desmond Leahy, Dr Tom Gumbrielle, Mrs Isabelle McNicholas, Dr Jack Sullivan, Father Frank Kelly, Mr Tom Arnold, Mrs Kay Kirwan, Mrs Margaret O'Loughlin, Mr Dermot MacDermott, Mrs Simone Hale, and the late Nurse Angela Buckley. The correspondence (1946–9) between some Irish staff members and the Théot family was also used.

— *a paper at a pathology meeting in Cambridge.* His eldest son, Patrick (1948–51), had been drowned a couple of months before; his widow, Ethna, was left with two sons under two years, and a daughter—the present author—who was born after the air crash. A scientist by training, Ethna Gaffney lectured in Chemistry at the RCSI, retiring as Professor of Chemistry in 1988. Both of Gaffney's surviving sons became doctors: the elder, Eoin, is like him a pathologist attached to TCD.

page 74 *'and of you and your family'.* Letter from Tommy Dunne to M. Théot, 15/9/49.

— *a poem entitled 'Mort de A.D.'.* For a discussion of the poem, see Harvey, pp. 230–4. Beckett and Darley were close friends at Saint-Lô: Dr Leahy recalls their frequent evenings spent down the town, followed by long discussions well into the night. (Telephone conversation with Dr Desmond Leahy, 30/9/98.)

— *'a town about the size of Saint-Lô'.* Letter from Timmy O'Driscoll to M. Théot, 9/11/47.

page 76 *stuck in the ruins of his house.* Lantier, p. 134; for other sources of inspiration, see Knowlson, pp. 475–6.

— *beautifully turned out in starched white blouses.* This is one abiding memory of an Irish woman, Mary Pat O'Malley (née Cullen), who visited the town in summer 1946. (Conversation, autumn 1997.)

— *which Beckett had helped to combat by procuring rat poison in Paris. Endgame,* London, Faber, 1958, p. 44, where Clov utters the unforgettable line: 'If I don't kill that rat he'll die'. Indeed, the role of Clov could conceivably be described as storekeeper and interpreter: he fetches items from the kitchen, knows when Hamm's painkillers have run out, and conveys messages to and from Hamm's parents. Towards the end of the play he exclaims on the expert attention given to the wounded who are dying.

— *'articles of faith which will resonate throughout his great works to come.'* Gordon, p. 201.

Notes to the English text

page 77 *a world abandoned by reason.* The many layers of allusions in the poem, and its relationship to the radio piece 'The Capital of the Ruins', will be discussed in a forthcoming publication by the author (*Irish University Review*, 29, 2, autumn/winter 1999).

— *a wider cross-section of the community than he had previously known.* Knowlson, p. 350.

— *'liberation through unspeakable suffering.'* Gordon, p. 192.

page 78 *a book of testimonies from grateful former patients and their relatives.* Gathered by the Saint-Lô Shanaghy Association, these handwritten recollections of the hospital were presented by members of the Association to the Irish Red Cross Society on 27 October 1998. (*Livre d'or.*)

— *never been adequately thanked for what they did.* A recurrent theme in the *Livre d'or* is the expression of regret on this score.

— *escaped the horrors of the war in Europe.* It should perhaps be added that the Normandy aid project drew on an area of expertise already well established in Ireland. As the former Irish Chief Medical Officer, James Deeny, remarks in his memoirs, 'one of the great achievements of this state since its foundation was the building of the hospitals.' (Deeny, p. 143.) Using funds from the sweepstakes, during the 1920s and 1930s the Irish Department of Local Government and Public Health had built and equipped over forty new hospitals to replace earlier buildings in poor repair.

— *'the nurses were always singing'.* One patient, aged five in 1945, remembers learning English nursery rhymes while being treated at the Irish Hospital. (*Livre d'or.*)

page 79 *'tact, diplomacy and kindness of the Irish hospital staff.'* Annick Mauduit, *Livre d'or.* (Translation by Jacqueline Fontanel.)

— *'many of us had never been abroad before.'* Beckett, 'the Capital of the Ruins', typescript, p. 3.

— *'These will have been in France.'* Beckett, 'The Capital of the Ruins', typescript, p. 4. A similar sentiment is expressed by Jim Gaffney, who was convinced of the positive effects of the experience for him: 'I feel, and so do the others, that a month's work here for people in need of our help is worth three months at home.' (JCG, letter to his brother Maurice, 10/9/45). Overall, he was aware of immeasurable benefits to be reaped: 'Looking up at the date I find it's two months since I came here; and I must add that I've learned more about humanity and human nature in these two months than I'd learn at home in two years.' (JCG, letter to his brother-in-law Christy Haugh, 28/10/45.)

Sources and bibliography

Archival sources

Archives départementales de la Manche, Saint-Lô
Archives municipales, Mairie, Saint-Lô
Croix-Rouge Française, Paris (CRF)
Faculty of Nursing, Royal College of Surgeons in Ireland (Mary Crowley's papers)
Irish Military Archives, Cathal Brugha Barracks, Dublin (Department of Defence)
Irish National Archives, Dublin (Departments of Finance, Foreign Affairs, Taoiseach)
Irish Red Cross Society Archives, Dublin (IRC)
Manuscripts Room, Trinity College Dublin Library
Mémorial Hospital, Saint-Lô
Ministère des Affaires Étrangères, Quai d'Orsay, Paris (files ZZ14–02, Z219–3, Z213–1,C60–1)
Musée du Bocage Normand, Ferme du Bois-Jugan, Saint-Lô
Saint-Lô Perth Committee, A. K. Bell Library, Perth

Bibliography

Anon., 'Je me souviens de l'hôpital irlandais. . .', *Manche Libre*, 12/10/1980
Arnold, Aidan, 'Samuel Beckett and the Irish Hospital in France', in *Lusk Through the Ages*, Lusk, Co. Dublin, Lusk Heritage Group, 1995, pp. 21–22
As No Other Dare Fail: For Samuel Beckett on His 80th Birthday by His Friends and Admirers, London, John Calder, and New York, Riverrun, 1986
Barrington, Ruth, *Health, Medicine and Politics in Ireland 1900–1970*, Dublin, Institute of Public Administration, 1987
Bataille de Normandie: official guide, Paris, Gallimard, 1994
Beckett, Samuel, 'The Capital of the Ruins', 10 June 1946 (radio broadcast, published by O'Brien, 1986, 1990; McMillan, 1986; and by Gontarski, 1995)
— 'Antipepsis', *Metre*, 3, Autumn 1997, p. 5
Beevor, Antony and Cooper, Artemis, *Paris after the Liberation: 1944–49*, Harmondsworth, Penguin, 1994

Sources and bibliography

Boivin, Michel, Bourdin, Gérard, Quellien, Jean, *Villes normandes sous les bombes (juin 1944)*, Caen, Presses Universitaires, 1994

Carroll, Joseph T., *Ireland in the War Years*, Newton-Abbott, David & Charles Ltd., 1975

Croix-Rouge Française: Bulletin d'information, Paris, 1944, 1945

Cronin, Anthony, *Samuel Beckett: The Last Modernist*, London, HarperCollins, 1996 (Flamingo paperback, 1997)

Deeny, James, *To Cure and to Care: Memoirs of a Chief Medical Officer*, Dún Laoghaire, Glendale, 1989

Department of Local Government and Public Health, *The Hospitals Commission First General Report 1933–4*, Dublin, Government Publications, 1936

Desile, Albert, 'L'histoire de l'hôpital irlandais', *Manche Libre*, 3/12/1978 and 17/12/1978

Desile, Albert, 'Un ancien de l'hôpital irlandais', *Manche Libre*, 28/9/1980

Fleetwood, John, 'An Irish Field-Ambulance in the Franco-Prussian War', *The Irish Sword*, VI, 1963–4, pp. 137–48

Florentin, Eddy, *La Bataille de Normandie*, Rennes, Ouest-France, 1993

France Croix-Rouge, Paris, 1946

Gaffney, Phyllis, '*Just* a quibble: a Note on Beckett's Handwriting', *French Studies Bulletin*, Winter 1997, pp. 16–17

— 'Why was Ireland given special treatment? The awkward state of Franco-Irish diplomatic relations, August 1944–March 1945', *Études Irlandaises*, 24–1, 1999 (spring) pp. 151–62

— 'Dante, Manzoni, de Valera, Beckett? Circumlocutions of a storekeeper: Samuel Beckett and Saint-Lô', *Irish University Review*, 29 (autumn/winter 1999)

Gontarski, S. E., (ed.) *Samuel Beckett: The Complete Short Prose, 1929–1989*, New York, Grove Press, 1995

Gordon, Lois, *The World of Samuel Beckett 1906–1946*, New Haven and London, Yale University Press, 1996

Gourbin, Bernard, *Les Inconnus célèbres de Normandie*, Paris, Albin Michel, 1995, pp. 253–9

Harvey, Lawrence E., *Samuel Beckett: Poet and Critic*, Princeton, Princeton University Press, 1970

Hayes-McCoy, G. A., 'The Irish Company in the Franco-Prussian War, 1870–71', *The Irish Sword*, I, 1949–53, pp. 275–83

Hutchinson, John F., *Champions of Charity: War and the Rise of the Red Cross*, Boulder and Oxford, HarperCollins, 1996

The Irish Hospitals Sweeps' Charitable Achievements, pamphlet, no date

Irish Independent, various articles, 1944–6
Irish Nurses' Organisation Souvenir Book, 1947
Irish Press, various articles, 1944–6
Irish Red Cross Monthly Bulletin, vols. 4–6, 1944–6
Irish Times, various articles, 1944–6
Keogh, Dermot, *Ireland and Europe 1919–1948*, Dublin, Gill and Macmillan, 1988
Knowlson, James, *Damned to Fame: The Life of Samuel Beckett*, London, 1996
Lantier, Maurice, *Saint-Lô au bûcher,* Condé-sur-Vire, 1993
— '*Histoire succincte du drame Saint-Lois*', in *44 Jours pour la Liberté*, a bilingual booklet produced by the Comité Saint-Lô 44, during the fiftieth anniversary commemorations, June/July 1994, pp. 20-21
Leeson, M. A., *Reminiscences of the Franco-Irish Ambulance; or, our 'corps' with the Mocquarts and on the Loire 1870-1871*, Dublin, McGlashan & Gill, 1873
Lefrançois, Auguste-Louis, *Quand Saint-Lô voulait revivre (juillet à Noël* 1944*)*, Coutances, 1947
Lelièvre, Raymond, '*Dans nos ruines . . . une cité blanche: l'hôpital irlandais de Saint-Lô, don de l'Irlande à la Normandie*', *Terre Normande*, série 1, no. 3, March-April 1946, p. 14.
McKinney, Colonel T. J., 'The Army Medical Service', in *The Call to Arms: A Historical Record of Ireland's Defence Services*, Dublin, Abbey publications, 1945, pp. 51–55
— '*L'hôpital irlandais de Saint-Lô*', *Terre Normande*, série 1, no. 3, March–April 1946, p. 15
McMillan, Dougald, 'Beckett at Forty: the Capital of the Ruins and Saint-Lô', and 'The Capital of the Ruins', in *As No Other Dare Fail*, pp. 67–70 and pp. 71–76
McNamara, Martin, 'The Origin and Development of the Irish Red Cross Society', in *The Call to Arms: A Historical Record of Ireland's Defence Services*, Dublin, Abbey publications, 1945, pp. 205–214
Manche Libre, various articles (Saint-Lô edition), 1945, 1946
Manche 1945: À travers nos ruines, brochure published by the Amis de la Manche, edited by Raoul Dabèse, Louis Racel, Joseph-Alexandre Leclerc, Paris, 1945
Mémorial de la Libération de Saint-Lô, 6 juin 1944, Saint-Lô, Imprimerie de Basse-Normandie et Digard Gotshaux Conseil, 1974
O'Brien, Eoin, *The Beckett Country*, Dublin, London and New York, the Black Cat Press in association with Faber and Faber, 1986
— 'Samuel Beckett at Saint-Lô—"Humanity in Ruins"', *Journal of the Irish Colleges of Physicians and Surgeons*, vol. 19, No. 2, April 1990,

Sources and bibliography

pp. 137–45

O'Regan, John and Dearey, Nicola (eds.), *Michael Scott Architect: in (casual) conversation with Dorothy Walker*, Kinsale, Gandon, 1995

O'Shea, Fionan, 'Doctors for Export', *The Bell*, 2, 2, May 1941, pp. 47–57

Ouest-France, various articles (Saint-Lô edition), 1946, 1956

Patry, Robert, *Saint-Lô: la Capitale des Ruines*, with an English translation by Eugène Turboult, *A Guide to Saint-Lô and the Battle Area*, Saint-Lô, Syndicat d'Initiative, 1948

Revue internationale de la Croix-Rouge, Geneva, 1945, 1946

Rioux, Jean-Pierre, *La France de la Quatrième République, vol. 1: L'ardeur et la nécessité 1944–1952*, Paris, Seuil, 1980

Ryan, Cornelius, 'Bombed St. Lô seemed only a bus stop away', *Sunday Independent*, 17/1/60

Témoignages des Saint-Lois de 44, booklet published by the Association Saint-Lô 44, Saint-Lô, 1994

Van Hoek, Kees, 'Irish Newsletter', *Sunday Express*, 7/7/46

Webb, Arthur, *The Clean Sweep: the Story of the Irish Hospitals Sweepstake*, London, Harrap, 1968

Conversations/interviews

Arnold, Tom, telephone conversation, September 1997
Buckley, Angela, Newbridge, 9 May 1997
Carroll, Nessa, telephone conversation, January 1998
Corcoran, (Mrs) Freddie, Dublin, October 1997
Daguts, Marcel, Saint-Lô, March 1998
Fitzgerald, Meave, Dublin, 7 February 1998
Gumbrielle, Tom, telephone conversations, May and June 1998
Hale, Simone, Dublin, 10 June 1997
Interview with former patients and employees of the hospital, organised by the Shanaghy Association, Musée du Bocage Normand, Bois-Jugan, Saint-Lô, 17 May 1997
Kelly, Frank, telephone conversation, March 1998
Leahy, Desmond, Dublin, 31 August and (telephone conversations) 2, 30 September 1998; 5, 6, 7, October 1998
Maguire, Peter, Dublin, 29 April 1997
MacMahon, Jacqueline, Dublin, March 1997
Menant, Marcel, Saint-Lô, 17 and 19 May 1997
Mulloy, Sheila, Dublin, November 1997
McKee, Simone, Saint-Lô, March 1998
O'Loughlin, Margaret, Dublin, March 1998

O'Rahilly, Blánaid, Dublin, 7 February 1998
Smith, Louis, telephone conversation, February 1998
Théot, Marie-Anne, Saint-Lô, several occasions, 1996–8
Villechalane, Paulette, Saint-Lô, 17 May 1997

Unpublished sources

Barrett, Marguerite, autograph album and scrap book
Beckett, Samuel, letters to Thomas MacGreevy, 19/8/45 and 21/12/45, TCD Library, Manuscripts Room (ms. 10402)
— Postcard to Irish Red Cross, 5/2/87 (IRC Archives)
Boland, Tim, letters to the Théots, 14/1/47; 6/4/47; 21/12/47
Buckley, Angela, photograph album and scrap book
Crowley, Mary, 'The Irish Red Cross Hospital, Saint-Lô', report to accountant, 29/8/46
— 'The story of the *hôpital irlandais, Saint-Lô*', 1/4/48
— 'The *hôpital irlandais, Saint-Lô*: address to the Soroptimist Club of Dublin', 23/11/48
— set of her papers relating to the Saint-Lô hospital, lent to the author by Bridie Walsh
Darley, Arthur, letter to Monsieur Théot, 30/12/1946
Desramé, David, *Les cités de la mémoire: ethnologie mise en valeur*, postgraduate thesis, Department of Social Anthropology, University of Caen, 1994
Dunne, Tommy, letters to the Théots, 9/2/47; 4/1/48; 15/9/49
Gaffney, James Cyril, letters from Saint-Lô to members of his family, August 1945–August 1946 (abbreviated as JCG)
Irish Red Cross Central Council Minutes, vols. 2 and 3
Irish Red Cross Executive Committee Minutes, No. 2
Irish Red Cross Miscellaneous Minute Books (1940–9)
Kergorlay, de, Brigitte, letter to the author, 4/8/97
Kergorlay, de, Denis, letter to the author, 17/6/97
Killick, Beryl and Michael, letter to the Théots, 15/11/50
Leahy, Desmond, fax communications to the author, 27/3/98, 15/4/98 and 26/6/98
Livre d'or: over five hundred handwritten appreciations and memories of the Irish Hospital, gathered in and around Saint-Lô from former patients and their relatives, mainly by Madame Marie-Anne Théot of the Shanaghy Association, Saint-Lô, 1996–8
MacDermott, Maeve, autograph album
MacMahon, Jacqueline, autograph album
McNicholas, Isabelle, letter to the author, 22/7/98
McNicholas, Paddy, letter to the Théots, 23/10/47

Sources and bibliography

O'Driscoll, Tim, letter to the Théots, 9/11/47
Ryan, Richard, 'On Irish Ambulance Corps, Franco-Prussian War 1870' (*c.* 1910–15), typescript
Ville de Saint-Lô: Délibérations du Conseil Municipal, années 1944–1947, t. 1 (Archives of the *Mairie*, Saint-Lô: *Archives municipales*)

INDEX

A

affaire de l'hôpital irlandais, 56, 57–70

B

Bardeck, Fr 53
Barrett, Marguerite 36, 75
Beckett, Samuel
  20, 26, 28, 32, 33, 35, 37, 39, 50, 52, 53, 55, 68, 74–7, 79
  Beckettian landscape of bombed Saint-Lô 12
  epigraphs quoting 1, 15, 28, 43, 57, 71
  gift for Tommy Dunne 41
  interpreter, as 25, 29
  leaves hospital, 40–1
  literary works and career 40, 75, 77
    'Antipepsis' (poem) 76
    En Attendant Godot (Waiting for Godot) 75
    Fin de Partie (Endgame) 75, 76
    Happy Days 76
    'Saint-Lô' (poem) 76
    'The Capital of the Ruins' (radio talk) 46, 76
  storekeeper, as 25, 29, 30
Boland, Tim 38, 51, 73
  Dáil candidate for Kildare 73
Bon Sauveur hospital 6, 13
Bourdon, Jean 13, 51, 64–9
Buckley, Angela 37, 51, 52, 75

C

Caen 6
Café des Ruines 48
Canisey 28
Carey, Patrick 41, 50, 73
Centre Hospitalier Mémorial France États-Unis 72, 77
Collins, Fr 60
Collis, Robert 33
Conroy, Kathleen 38, 75
Coutances 10, 11, 13, 53, 64
Coutainville, villa at 52–3
Couvez, Daniel 50
Cranbourne, Lord 16
Croix-rouge française (see Red Cross, French)
Crowley, Mary 20–21, 39, 45, 58, 74
Cunningham, Nora 38

D

D-Day 1, 5, 7
Daly, Comdt C. J. 22
Dautry, Raoul 11, 23
Darley, Arthur 24, 26, 41–2, 51, 55–6, 73
de Flavigny, Count 19
de Gaulle, Charles 11, 17–19, 22
  visits Saint-Lô 11
de Gromard, Jacqueline 73
de Kergorlay, Countess 28
de Kergorlay, Comte 52–3
de Valera, Eamon 63
Delannoë, Cécile 51

Deschevaux-Dumesnil, Suzanne 25
Desile, Albert 40, 47
Dieppe 32, 49
  Hôtel des Arcades 32
Digan, Al 74
Dillon, Douglas 72
Doherty, Margaret 38
Dunne, Tommy 26, 41, 73, 74

E

Entr'Aide Francaise 66

F

Fahey, Dilly 75
Fahy, Mrs 21
Fitzgerald, Maurice 32–3, 36
Fitzgerald, Meave 33
Fitzpatrick, Mary 38
Franco-Prussian War (1870–71) 33

G

Gablin, Louis 65
Gaffney, Jim 24–5, 26, 28–32, 33, 34–5, 36, 37, 38, 39, 40, 41, 43, 47, 51–56, 58–60, 63, 73, 78
Gennevilliers 40
German forces 1, 4–9
  confiscate radios 12
  counter-offensive 7
  organise exodus from Saint-Lô 9
  surrender of 10
  tanks 4
German prisoners of war 30–2, 47
Gordon, Lois 77
Granville 37, 53
Gumbrielle, Edward (Ned) 39, 74

H

Hackett, Mrs 21
Healy, Terry 74
Hilt, André 11
Hynds, Fr Brendan 39, 43, 74

I

Irish Ambulance Unit (1870) 19
Irish Hospital Sweepstakes 16, 62
Irish Minister to France, the 44, 63 (see also Murphy, Seán)
Irish Press 19, 59–60
Irish Times, The 76

K

Killick, Michael 26, 75
Knowlson, James 77

L

Lafont, M. 24, 47, 52
Lavalley, Georges 11, 56, 63–6, 68–70, 72
Le Hutrel 8
Leahy, Desmond 33–4, 37, 50–53, 59, 63, 74
Lecluse, Rosalie 51
Lecouillard, Dr 13
Lefèvre, Simone 73
Lefrançois, Auguste-Louis 10, 11, 14
Lelièvre, Raymond 38, 64
Lerebourg, Maurice 47
Lippitt, Dr 31
livre d'or 78

M

Ma Normandie (song) 70, 75
MacAuley, C. J. 63
MacDermott, Ita Maeve 38, 75
MacGreevy, Thomas 40, 55

MacWhite, Michael 60
Maguire, Conor 61
Malone, Margaret 74
Manche Libre 47, 57, 68, 71
Martin, Margaret 38
Mathieu, Georges 17
McKee, Frederick 24–6, 73
McKinney, Col Thomas 20–24, 26, 28, 30, 39, 52, 56, 59, 65, 66, 70, 72, 77
  wife dies 39
McMahon, Heber 73
McNamara, Martin, 16
McNicholas, Paddy 39, 45, 70, 74
médailles de la Reconnaissance française 77
Médecins sans Frontières 58
Menant, Marcel 34, 64
Mullally, Eileen 38
Murphy, Julia 38, 73
Murphy, Roderick 41
Murphy, Seán 17–18, 23, 44, 63

N

Nelson, Paul 72
Nos Vieux Pommiers (song) 75

O

O'Driscoll, Timmy 39, 74
Olden, Clare 36, 73
O'Rahelly, Breda 73
O'Reilly, Anne M. 38
Ouest-France 57, 68

P

Patton, General 4
Perth, Scotland
  adopts Saint-Lô 38
  French Association 38
Philippe, Albert 13, 64–69
Pilorget, Mme. 37, 53

Polish project 58, 59, 60

R

Radio Éireann 19, 46, 76, 79
Radiodiffusion française 12
rats 12, 37, 41, 76
Red Cross organisation 52
Red Cross, American 21
Red Cross, French 16, 17, 19, 22, 28, 35, 39, 43–4, 52, 58, 62, 65, 73
  President (see also Sicé, General Adolphe) 16, 17, 44, 65
  Secretary 16, 17
Red Cross, Irish 14–27, 33, 43, 45, 46, 57–67
  21 St Stephen's Green (headquarters) 20
  Anti-Tuberculosis campaign 61
  Chairman 44 (see also Maguire, Conor)
  continuing appeals for funds 61
  Dún Laoghaire refugee centre 15
  executive committee 63
  finances 61
  fundraising appeals 57
  home at Glencree 61
  mobile hospital unit proposal 16
  Operation Shamrock 15
  Secretary 16 (see also McNamara, Martin)
  uniforms, 16, 30, 52
  Warsaw project 58–61
Red Cross, Polish, 59
Royal College of Surgeons in Ireland 25
  Faculty of Nursing 75

S

Saint-Joseph hospital 13
Scott, Michael 22, 24, 59, 60
Sicé, General Adolphe 17
Smith, Dorothy 38
Stewart, George 32, 33, 36, 73
Stirling. E. M. 38
Sullivan, Kitty 42, 73, 74
Sunday Express 49

T

Théot family 48, 73–75
Théot, Madame 75
Thompson, Alan 20, 22, 24–6, 28, 30, 33, 53, 58, 74
Thompson, Geoffrey 20

V

Van Hoek, Kees 49
Verrières, Dr 13
Vichy regime 5, 17
Vire river 4, 13, 76